Choctaw-Apache Foodways

Choctaw-Apache Foodways

by
Robert B. Caldwell, Jr.

STEPHEN F. AUSTIN STATE UNIVERSITY PRESS
2015

For more information:

Stephen F. Austin State University Press

P.O. Box 13007 SFA Station

Nacogdoches, Texas 75962

sfapress@sfasu.edu

www.sfasu.edu/sfapress

Book design: Kirstie Linstrom, Teri Klauser

Distributed by Texas A&M Consortium

www.tamupress.com

LIBRARY OF CONGRESS CATALOGING-IN-PUBLICATION DATA

Caldwell, Jr., Robert B.

Choctaw-Apache Foodways / Robert B. Caldwell, Jr.

p.cm.

ISBN: 978-1-62288-099-7

FUNDING MADE POSSIBLE BY A GRANT FROM
CANE RIVER NATIONAL HERITAGE AREA

CONTENTS

Author's Note

I wrote the pages of this book, but the credit really goes to the Choctaw-Apache community of Sabine Parish, who both taught me what I know about this subject and whose families continue to pass down traditional foodways. This book was inspired foremost by my maternal great-grandparents, George and Susan Remedies, and my mother, Vickie Holbrook. Chief John W. Procell and the Choctaw-Apache Tribal Council of 2008-2011 supported my initial research and introduced me to a number of excellent traditional cooks. Chairman Jason Rivers and my fellow council members 2011-2013 continued that support. Rhonda Remedies Gauthier has been an invaluable source of information and encouragement. She has helped with every aspect of this book from initial idea to completion. In this and other projects she has been the best research partner anyone could ask for.

This book grew from my M.A. Thesis Project at Northwestern State University in Natchitoches, Louisiana. Dr. Hiram F. "Pete" Gregory, the chair

George and Susan Remedies. From author's personal collection.

of my M.A. Thesis committee, showed tireless patience and continues to provide mentorship to me. Dr. Susan Dollar, also on my committee, has offered corrections to my poor spelling, grammar, and punctuation. Archivist Mary Linn Wernett of the Cammie G. Henry Research Center has been helpful to me on numerous occasions. While many others have helped in the research and creation of this book, I take responsibility for all mistakes in it.

Choctaw-Apache Foodways is made possible through a grant from the Cane River National Heritage Area. While I attended Northwestern State University, I interned at Cane River National Heritage Area offices. I sincerely thank Cynthia Sutton and the staff of CRNHA for their consistent encouragement to complete this book and to continue my education in pursuit of the Ph.D.

Numerous friends and family members helped in most every way imaginable at some point of this research and writing. Thank you as well. If I failed to acknowledge you in some way, or wrote your recipe down wrong, please forgive this oversight.

Introduction

Food is an important marker of ethnicity, region, and even national identity. It has been used to delineate national and cultural boundaries, and to communicate social prestige or economic wealth. Food often serves an integral part of both individual and group identity. Sometimes, foods are simultaneously markers for more than one identity, and foods often create walls or borders around identity. People everywhere associate food with home, family and security, but it often takes on deeper communicative functions, conveying complex social messages.[1]

Priests, Louisa Toby; Joseph Hosea Procella; Mary Procella, Martha Toby Carmona & Dora Toby Garza about 1900. Private Collection. A copy of the photo is in the Ebarb Community Collection, Cammie G. Henry Archives NSULA.

This work examines the traditional food culture of the Choctaw-Apache community of Ebarb, located in Sabine Parish, Louisiana. Sabine Parish is in west-northwest Louisiana, and is bounded by Toledo Bend Reservoir (formerly Sabine River) to the west and Natchitoches Parish to the east. While western Sabine Parish has the densest geographical distribution of enrolled members of the tribe, the entire parish is a State Designated Tribal Statistical area for purposes of the U.S. Census.

The tribe traces its roots to Indians living in proximity to 18th-century Spanish and French colonial forts and missions, most notably the capital of Spanish Tejas at the presidio Nuestra Senora del Pilar de Los Adaes, the mission San Miguel de los Adeas, as well as to emancipated Lipan Apache slaves, and Choctaw bands that settled in the area around 1800. Recognized by the state of Louisiana in 1978, the Choctaw-Apache Tribe continues to seek federal acknowledgement from the Bureau of Indian Affairs, U.S. Department of the Interior. The tribe has over 3000 enrolled citizens. Ebarb and Zwolle have a combined tribal student population in excess of 700, and the public schools receive funding under Office of Indian Education programs, Department of Education.[2]

The Choctaw-Apache community has a

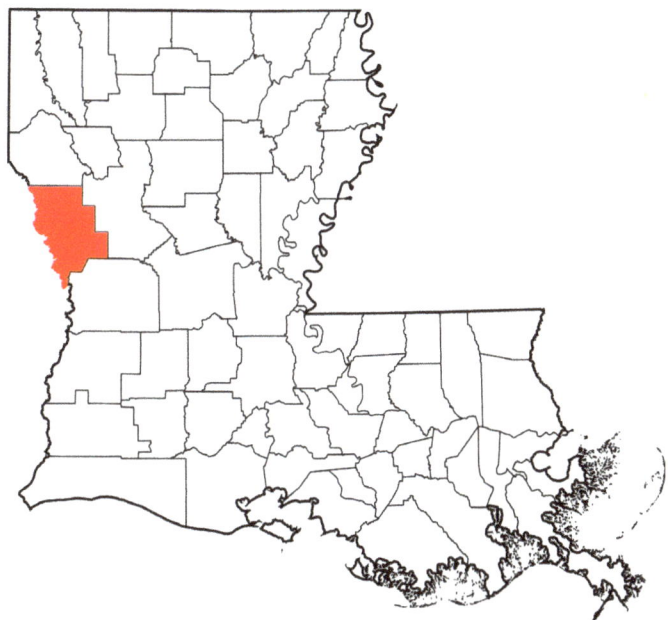

Map of Louisiana Highlighting Sabine Parish. Map by David Benbennick (public domain).

cultural heritage rich in food traditions, and the Tribe recognizes the importance of food as a part of their traditions.[3] These food traditions have long constituted an important ethnic marker for the community. However, these foodways are woefully understudied, even at "face value." Academic treatments of the Choctaw-Apache foodways as an investigation of ethnic identity are virtually non-existent.

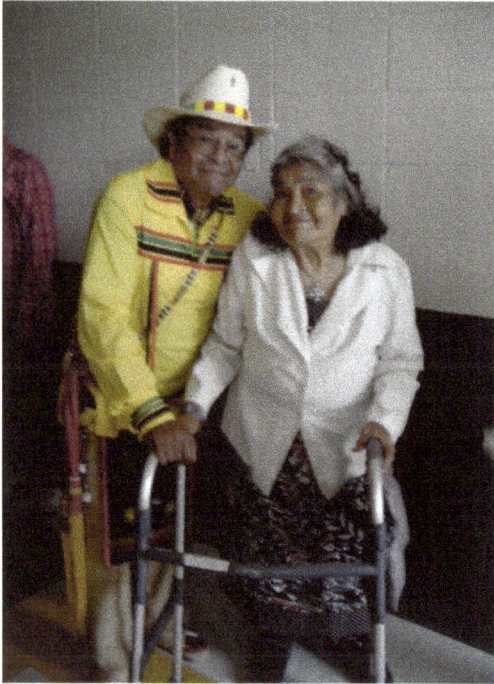

Chief John W. Procell and Esther Procell, 2010. Photo by the author.

The research and writing of this book presented both an amazing opportunity and several specific challenges. I am a member of the Choctaw-Apache Tribe, but grew up outside of the community. I am a student of history, anthropology, heritage resources and a lifelong food enthusiast. This book was created through a kind of "food dialogue" between the myself and other tribal members.[4] Beginning with the help Choctaw-Apache Chairman John W. Procell and the Tribal Council (the political representatives of the Tribe), I met with elder members of the community and other keepers of traditional food knowledge. I also relied heavily on word of mouth through my own extended family members and other community contacts to recruit people to share their food knowledge.

I draw heavily on the resources at the Louisiana Folklife Center and the Cammie G. Henry Research Center at Northwestern State University. The Folklife Center has demonstrated interest in documenting and preserving the foodways of the region, including those of the Choctaw-Apache Tribe and other "Adaesaño" (descendants of the Spanish-period Los Adaes fort and mission) populations, as attested by the Folklife Center's publication of "Making Tamales in Northwestern Louisiana," by Dayna Bowker Lee. The Center also supported a tamale-making demonstration at Los Adaes with Rhonda Remedies Gauthier and her father, the late John Remedies, and is the depository of photographs and papers related to that demonstration.

I first became interested in this topic after reading interviews of my great grandparents conducted in the early 1980s. Those interviews are part of a series of interviews from the early 1980s housed in the Ebarb Community Collection at Cammie G. Henry Research Center. The Ebarb Community Collection contains over 100 interview transcripts, twenty-five audio cassettes, and ten rolls of film. The interviews were conducted by Mennonite Central Committee volunteers Janet Shoemaker and Mary Van Rheenen. Their presence was part of a mostly secular, broad community aid plan devoted to assist in community-controlled projects.

The book also builds on Traditional Arts and Crafts in

Beto Castie (Castillo) born Aug 5, 1896. Photo ca. 1945. Betty Lucille Rivers Collection.

the Choctaw-Apache Community of Ebarb (1996), a project which was undertaken by the tribe and supported by the Louisiana Division of the Arts, and other relevant studies. One of my goals is to offer the Tribe additional documentation of the foodways of our American Indian culture as well as new physical and analytical resources on this important aspect of ethnic identity.

Thus far, most attention on this community's foods has been focused on the tamale. Publications have generally taken the form of documentation and/or recipes, but they invariably lack historical context, critical examination, or other detailed interpretation. This book incorporates additional foods and places the totality of tribal foodways in historical context while considering the relationship between food and ethnic identity. In doing so, the project offers a framework for further investigation, documentation, and reflexive examination by members of the Tribe. This book also offers an alternative model to the "straightforward" foodlore and cookbook data gathering that is prevalent among those exploring the world of food heritage. In doing so, this book aims to bring broader public awareness to the Native American foodways of the region and to serve as a reference resource for the tribe.

Subsistence garden crops and animals commonly raised in the community before 1980 are considered in this book, as are foods that were hunted, trapped, and fished, and plants that have been wild gathered I also include some food preparation tools and techniques that have been used among Choctaw-Apache families. This book continues a long-standing discussion regarding the power that the food tradition holds in reinforcing and interrogating tribal identity in the community. Meals, fasting, feasting, and food reciprocity serve to reinforce Choctaw-Apache identity, while many argue that symbols associated with the Tamale Fiesta have served to obscure indigenous identity.

While food has a central place in reinforcing group identity and culture, it is also an ethnic marker. As such, it creates a boundary against, and a bridge to outsiders. This book includes recipes but is meant to be much more than a cookbook. It is history. It is ethnography. The research also seeks to offer readers a comparative point with the foods of other closely related tribes and cultural groups.

At the same time, this study does not address any and all foods eaten by community members. For example, the book does not consider the social meaning of pizza to tribal youth, nor does it directly address the relationship of fast foods to eroding ethnic solidarity. I focus on the traditional foods that help constitute community identity. Traditional foods might include old family recipes, foods eaten by interviewees' parents and grandparents, natural and low-processed foods which were historically produced by local agriculture, hunting, and food gathering.[5]

The traditional food knowledge of the Choctaw-Apache community has been transmitted orally and through practice for generations. Children learned how to make foods from their older siblings, parents and grandparents by watching and listening. But my investigation required me to follow the "paper trail" to provide sufficient context.

Food & the Choctaw-Apache in a Scholarly Context

Clark Wissler opened his classic The American Indian: An Introduction to the Anthropology of the New World noting, "the most tangible and objective of human traits are those dealing with food."[6] That insight – despite subsequent waves of food "globalization"– is no less true today. As Linda Berzok explains, foodways are particularly resistant to change.[7] This certainly applies to the Choctaw-Apache community.

Anthropologists have long looked at food habits and various rituals surrounding food. More than one hundred years ago, Frank Hamilton Cushing, anthropology's first participant observer, published Zuñi Breadstuff in serial form (1884-1885). Wissler wrote about American Indian foods more encyclopedically, expressing foods' relations to the bio-regions of North America. Claude Levi-Strauss, in his pivotal Raw and the Cooked (1966) and From Honey to Ashes (1973), analyzed myth – including food dichotomies among New World tribal peoples – to look at what could be an underlying universal structural thought. K.C Chang's Food in Chinese Culture (1977) offers an excellent model for looking at food as cultural heritage from a combined historical and anthropological perspective. More recently, Everyone Eats: Understanding Food and Culture, by E.N. Anderson (2005), addresses the biological and cultural aspects of food, providing useful insights into food origins and diffusion and food as communication. Anderson's book offers an invaluable framework for food as a cultural marker and discusses ethnic borders, food as traditional medicine, and foodway change.

The Southern United States leads the way in the study of food and heritage, boasting the Southern Foodways Alliance at Oxford, Mississippi, and the Southern Food and Beverage Museum in New Orleans, Louisiana. Those institutions inspire the tastebuds, but also the mind. The study of "foodways" is a multi-disciplinary endeavor, and some cookbooks contextualize their recipes within broader food culture. Chef John Folse's numerous cookbooks, replete with detailed historical and cultural background, inspire this food book project.

While food history and culture have enjoyed a recent resurgence in scholarship and popular interest, study of American food culture was out of vogue for decades. Academics ignored traditional American Indian foods from the 1930s until the 1970s. As a consequence, many twentieth-century books on American Indian foods lack intellectual rigor. These books can be divided into one or more of the following: broad overviews usually written for a general audience, specific case studies, "how to" books (including gardening), and cookbooks. Since Wissler, many writers have retained breadth but lacked detail and specificity in their food surveys. Scores of general overviews recite the oft-told story of the "three-sisters" (maize, beans, and squash) gardens and wild game but are too broad to accurately describe any specific American Indian community. One very notable exception to the mediocrity in this category is Linda Murray Berzok's American Indian Food (1997). This book is by far the best and most-accessible overview of American Indian foods from a scholarly perspective. It tends toward historical particulars, but, in addition to its historical overview, the book includes chapters on food preparation and storage; food customs; food and religion; and indigenous concepts of diet and nutrition. In the twenty first century, scholarly interest in American Indian foods is growing. Many excellent works have been published over the past fifteen years. The best recent overview of American Indian foods in the U.S. south is Rayna Green's "Mother Corn and the Dixie Pig" (2008) published in Southern Cultures.

Other books concentrate on case studies. Examples range from academic works, like Frank Hamilton Cushing's classic Zuni Breadstuff and James Vlasich's Pueblo Indian Agriculture (2005), to books self-published by tribes and community cookbooks. "How to" books include gardening and wild food foraging books also abound. Gary Paul Nabhan's Enduring Seeds: Native American Agriculture and Wild Plant Conservation (1989) is the best of such books, linking food sovereignty to tribal sovereignty and issuing a clarion call for the preservation of existing native seeds through seed banks. These books are useful, when combining a demonstration garden with heritage education, for encouraging family-level gardening revitalization, and encouraging the continuation of harvesting wild plants for medicine and food.

Cookbooks might be further subdivided into three broad categories: those with an "historical"/traditional emphasis, those that rely on traditional recipes but make accommodations to modern ingredients, measurements and techniques; and those with modern recipes loosely based on Native American ingredients.[8] Some books simultaneously perpetuate harmful stereotypes and offer useful information. For example, the 1977 booklet Indian Cookin', by Herb Walker includes a drawing of a stereotypical "Indian girl" cooking and an ear of corn on the cover, but its introduction includes a surprisingly good overview of spices and seasonings. Yeffe Kimball and Jean Anderson's The Art of American Indian Cooking (1965) offers hundreds of American Indian recipes adapted for the growing mass-markets of the 1960s. The book's ingredient lists include beef and chicken bouillon cubes, butter (and buttermilk), frozen meats, etc. But the book does not tackle the question of cultural change, thus treating the recipes as timeless. However, the authors do a decent job of dividing the recipes into regionally-based chapters. The book's chapter on the Southwest region— which is most useful to this project— features tamales, tortillas, green pepper and beans. Beverly Cox and Martin Jacobs's Spirit of the Harvest: North American Indian Cooking (1991) is a beautifully illustrated "coffee table" cookbook that focuses on "gourmet interpretations" of selected foods. While the book lacks tribal specificity, its beautiful photographs remind readers of the importance of drawing on the sense of sight to evoke their imagination of smell and taste.

To date no book-length academic history or detailed ethnography has been written on the Choctaw-Apache of Ebarb. Dr. Hiram F. Gregory is undoubtedly the most knowledgeable academic authority on the tribe, having written numerous short pieces focusing on various aspects of the community, and alluding to the community in longer papers and entries. In 1986, Gregory and John R. Faine co-authored The Apache-Choctaw of Ebarb: An Assessment of the Status of a Louisiana Indian Tribe, published by the Institute for Indian Development. The historical background section includes a timeline from 1719 to the 1980s and explains the social construction of racial identity in the Spanish Colonial era and beyond. The bulk of the report examines the health and welfare of the tribal statistical area from a medical and sociological point of view. Its health conclusions are useful in considering implications of traditional and contemporary foods on the community members' health. Similarly, Joan Marie Roche's Sociocultural Aspects of Diabetes in an Apache-Choctaw Community in Louisiana (1982) considers food-related health. Also, with Fred Kniffen and George Stokes, Gregory wrote The Historical Indian Tribes of Louisiana from 1542 to the Present, mentioning the tribe and providing dynamics of 18th-century Choctaw migration to, and settlement in, Louisiana. Both Mary B. Van Rheenan and Janet Shoemaker collected oral histories from the Choctaw-Apache Community in the early 1980s as part of a project with the Mennonite Central Committee. Those recordings have a wealth of food-related information.

Recent historical and archaeological publications help shed light on the context in which the Choctaw-Apache community formed. Captives and Cousins: Slavery, Kinship, and Community in the

Southwest Borderlands by James Brooks is useful in understanding Spanish borderlands generally and the trade in Apache slaves more specifically. In Changing National Identities at the Frontier: Texas and New Mexico, 1800-1850, Andrés Reséndez tackles the difficult questions of shifting ethnicity, self-identity, and national allegiance on the Spanish frontier lands in the early 19th-century, as well as the relationships of tribes and mixed indigenous populations and their relationship to colonial national powers. These historical dynamics helped instill a wide ranging food tradition in historical times, but also continues to impact the Choctaw-Apache community in numerous ways today.

Choctaw-Apache culture developed in relation to Los Adaes and along the El Camino Real de los Tejas, the major road through the Spanish colonial period ultimately linking Natchitoches, Louisiana to Mexico City. George Avery offered a wealth of historical information in his annual Los Adaes Station Archaeology Program reports. James L. McCorkle, Jr., has contributed articles on the history of Los Adaes, while Francis X. Galán's 2006 dissertation, Last Soldiers, First Pioneers: The Los Adaes Border Community on the Louisiana-Texas Frontier, 1721-1779, is the most detailed recent history of Los Adaes, unpacking nearly sixty years of history at and around the fort and mission. Galán's dissertation includes a limited overview of Adais foodways during the period. A running theme of Galán's dissertation is food scarcity at the fort, and trade between the Spanish presidio at Los Adaes, various tribes, and the French post Natchitoches.

The foodways of the Choctaw-Apache are understudied and, prior to this book, no focused study has been conducted. However, there are some important prior works directly pertaining to the topic. Most notably, this project continues the direction of Traditional Arts and Crafts in the Choctaw-Apache Community of Ebarb, which features community members making green pepper (and eggs), tamales, sausage (chorizo), and roasting ear, or "pondalote" bread (pan de elote). The publication also profiles community members' hunting and fishing, crafts, farming practices, and other aspects of tribal heritage.

Heritage is itself contested space.[9] In the United States, collective memory is a powerful tool of cultural survival, but it is often distorted in service to dominant culture, corporations and the state.[10] If history is a battlefield, then heritage is the redoubt from which different groups defend their class and other social group interests. Moreover, the meaning of cultural heritage has expanded over time to include intangible cultural heritage. In 2003, UNESCO adopted the Convention for the Safeguarding of the Intangible Cultural Heritage in order to "to safeguard the practices, representations, expressions, knowledge and skills that communities, groups and, in some cases, individuals recognize as part of their cultural heritage." Intangible cultural heritage represents practices that are traditional, contemporary and living, and "[w]hile fragile, intangible cultural heritage is an important factor in maintaining cultural diversity in the face of growing globalization." For American Indian tribes and other indigenous peoples, intangible cultural heritage is key to cultural survival. Food (including food procurement, traditional cooking practices, eating, and food-related division of labor) is an important example of intangible culture heritage.[11]

Sovereignty, deep ties to traditional cultural places, and heritage are paramount in most American Indian communities. This is true for the Choctaw-Apache of Ebarb. But when examining a tribe's ethnohistory and cultural ecology, researchers must resist tendency toward essentialist or teleological notions. This book examines the actual foods of the people by highlighting living traditions and living memories, rather than relegating the community to some idealized and long-forgotten past.

George Pierre Castille and Gilbert Kushner's edited volume Persistent People: Cultural Enclaves in Perspective (1981) addresses the processes of cultural enclavement, examining continuity of identity primarily as a form of resistance to absorption by a dominant surrounding culture. The Ebarb community has been described by Gregory and others as an endogamous cultural enclave.[12] While this book is not focused on precisely delineating the geographical boundaries of the Choctaw-Apache foodways, the pattern of cultural enclavement is evident in the foodways' sharp contrast to neighboring Anglo-American and African-American food traditions.

Stephen Cornell, in "The Transformations of Tribe: Organization and Self-concept in Native American Ethnicities" argues that group formation of collective identities – of both social and political scope – have been forming and reforming throughout time, and that invasion had profound effects on these identities. He traces identities along two axes: the conceptual (self-identification) and the political (group organization). Both of these are negotiated in relation to other groups. Where power differentials are high, they are often shaped by outsiders, often splitting the two dimensions apart. The American Indian community in western Sabine Parish areas has long experienced such challenges *vis-à-vis* dominant forces. Three hundred years of colonialism profoundly impacted the region. Spanish, French, Mexican, Texan, Confederate, and American governments foisted their own ascriptive identities onto the community.

It would be a serious oversight for any researcher to discuss food, ethnic identity, and heritage without considering class. The median income for members of the tribe is lower than the state average income,[13] but tribal members have long utilized the natural environment for hunting, fishing, and farming to supplement grocery store food. Until dispossession of "free range" common grazing land by the flooding of Sabine River, hogs and cattle were the backbone of community foods. Foodstuffs have long been traded within and beyond the community, and prepared foods are usually seen as a form of hospitality in most American Indian communities.[14] This explains the paucity of American Indian restaurants. Tamales have been one staple of the community for hundreds of years, as evidenced by *metate* fragments used to make *masa*.[15] According to Dorothy Remedies Harper, tamales were sold by women who made them in their homes since at least the 1950s. In recent decades, however, these tamales have become highly commodified. A tamale factory with a corporate structure and implementation of mechanical mass production and sale outside the community as well as the Zwolle Tamale Fiesta, a tourist-oriented festival initiated by outsiders beginning in the 1970s attest to this commodification. This began a contradictory process that simultaneously celebrated an important local indigenous food, while at the same time denied the food's rootedness in a centuries-old local tradition. Zwolle Tamale Fiesta promoters continue to draw upon popular 20th-century Mexican stereotypes that obscure the indigenous tamale's origins. In doing so, festival organizers have alienated some of the region's American Indian people.

However, individuals and groups combat their individual and collective alienation in many ways. Many recent studies suggest that participation in festivals, community gardens, farmers markets, and the like, offers a means by which to combat that alienation.[16] Likewise, geographer David Harvey has suggested that organizing around the "commons" is central to any struggle against further dispossession and rebuilding a sense of belonging and collectivity. These concepts can be applied in some way to this rural tribal community. Conceptualizing modern corporate-capitalist alienation in this way provides tools both to understand the world of the Choctaw-Apache (including why some tamale *makers* prefer to create hand-daubed tamales over machine-made ones) and to offer a method for political action that draws on tribal community gardens, seed banks, and historically-rooted food festivals to challenge alienation collectively. Lastly, amplifying the little-told story of Choctaw-Apache foodways offers me the opportunity—as researcher—to make a modest contribution to the ongoing task of decolonizing the academic fields in which I was trained.

Choctaw-Apache 2014 Powwow

A Note on Methodology

Using cross-disciplinary research, I drew upon written publications (history, cookbooks, ethnohistory, geography, literature, folklore, and archaeological reports), manuscripts, and other archive materials. The research hinged on participant observation with more than thirty contacts, oral history interviews, and community mapping.

Individual members of the tribe—and their families— displayed a wealth of information on the foodways of the community, but much of their knowledge is tacit. People see their knowledge as "everyday," or as "common sense," rather than part of a body of larger corpus of traditional indigenous knowledge. Additionally, much of their knowledge is fragmented. Some of the food-related wisdom hasn't been transmitted; therefore, older people tend to know more about traditional foods than their children or grandchildren. Some has been lost altogether. Because of the gendered division of labor, some knowledge is traditionally "male" while other knowledge is the purview of women. In a sense, this book collects the seeds of that knowledge from the various community members to create a "seed bank" of knowledge. That "seed bank" of human knowledge allows for diversity while aiming at an overall cultural synthesis.

Indigenous Foods

I contend that the distinct traditional foods of the Zwolle-Ebarb community are indigenous foods. But what is an indigenous food? What makes a food indigenous? The traditional foods of the area are actually both American Indian and colonial in origin. Like other forms of culture, foods might be assimilated, blended, rejected, or reinterpreted by a group.

From a biological perspective, indigenous foods are foods that are part of a food ecology. In North America, the pre-Columbian foods (often called "first foods," eaten at the time of, or previous to, European invasion provide one way to conceptualize indigenous foods. Corn, beans, and squash, tomatoes, pumpkin, pecans, black walnuts, blueberries, blackberries, deer and turkey are some indigenous foods in this sense.

Another way to understand indigenous foods is through a cultural lens. In this sense, the foods long-utilized by tribes are also indigenous foods. Some of these foods have been raised and cooked by American Indians for hundreds of years. For example, pork is such an integral part of Choctaw culture that, according to their legends, the pig has always been with them. Even the name for Choctaw folk tales, *Shukha Anumpa* ("pig tales"), illustrates the centrality of the pig in Choctaw culture. Likewise, sheep are central to Navajo culture. For hundreds of years, tribes have eaten chicken, grown watermelon, peaches, garlic, and a near-endless list of foods with European, African and Asian origins. These foods are now part of a historical, typical, festival, or in the case, of frybread, even stereotypical American Indian diet, just as tomatoes and potatoes of the Americas have come to be central to Eurasian cuisines (What is Italian food without the tomato?). Frybread is made from flour and cooked in oil. Nothing about it is pre-Columbian, but it is without dispute a traditional indigenous food throughout much of Indian Country. For the Choctaw-Apache community, some of the foods were introduced by the Spanish and French colonists over two hundred years ago, and incorporated into the indigenous diet. Other foods came after the arrival of Anglo-Americans.

Some important foods with European origins:

Pork
Beef
Chicken
White (wheat) flour
Many "wild" grapes, peaches, pears
Figs

Some important foods with African origins:

Black-eyed (including purple-hull) peas
Okra
Watermelon
Guinea fowl

Food Areas

Choctaw-Apache foodways are influenced by numerous cultural regions and ecological niches (river bottomland, southern forests, plains, desert) along the *Camino Real de los Tejas* (northeastern Mexico, Texas, Louisiana) and the culture region of the U.S. Southeast, as well as hundreds of years of cultural interactions between so-called "old world" and indigenous groups.

The Choctaw-Apache community is located at an ancient crossroads, a borderland area where the division between the numerous streams and bayous of Louisiana and the old prairies of Texas is now hidden in a dense pine forest. Anthropologists have long divided American Indian cultures into southeastern and southwestern cultural areas. Once again, the Choctaw-Apache represent a distinct mix of these "food areas."

Culture Areas of North America from "North American Indians of the Plains" by Clark Wissler. Popular Science Monthly, Vol. 82 May 1913.

C O R N

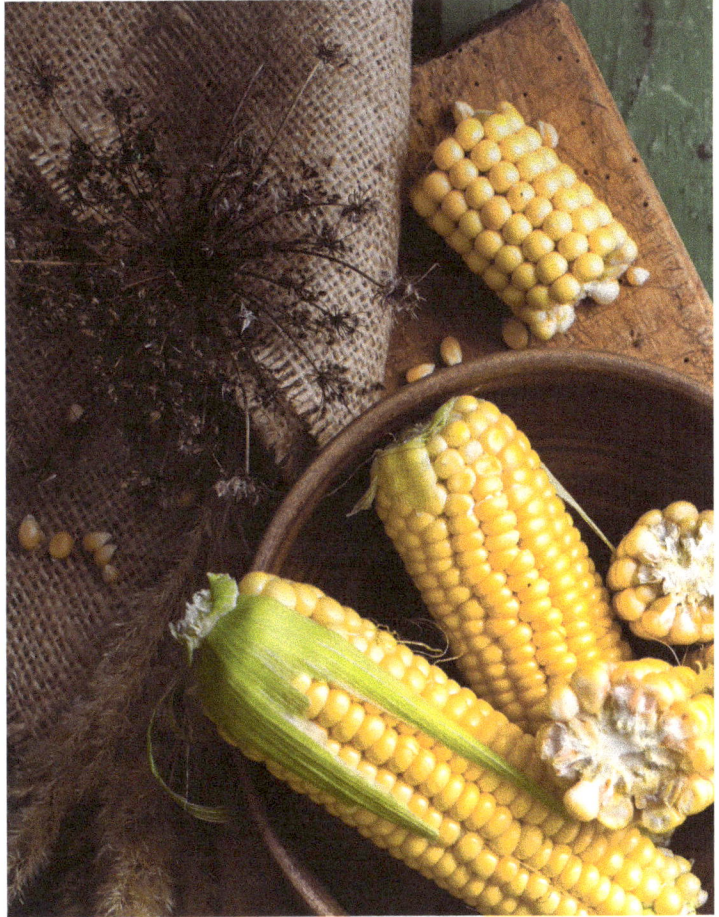

Corn

The corn complex is an indispensable component of Choctaw-Apache food traditions. Corn was such an important part of the tribe's culture that, according to Rhonda Remedies Gauthier, many families grew two seasons of corn every year.

Corn can be eaten fresh on the cob (boiled or roasted), canned, dried and made into hominy, grits, turned into dough, made into griddlebread or flatbreads, fried, used for tamale filling, and used as animal feed. Marjorie Remedies (widow of Ben Remedies), of Many, listed additional corn foods in a 2010 interview: "Fried cornbread, hot water cornbread, pones…[and] cornbread cakes." In addition to sweet corn, grinding corn, and corn for feed, many elders have attested to growing red popcorn.

Corn in the Field. Photo by the author.

Many families made flatbreads and griddle cakes. Those could be made from fresh corn, cornmeal, or *masa*. In 1983, Verna Sepulvado Ebarb explained how to make "corn cakes" and "metate bread":

You make your dough like this (for the tamales), but you don't put shortening in it for tortillas. You put in some salt, mix it with water, but don't put in any shortening….You can eat them with anything you want like other bread. When Momma was growing up, that's all they had for breakfast 'cause it's easy made…You can also make another kind of bread. They call it metate bread… you make up dough like hot tamales. Then take it and make it kind of oval shaped. Pat it about 1 ½ inch thick. Take and put that in a bread pan. You could make three little loaves or make it solid. It's the cheapest bread to make. And good for you.

A.J. Remedies explained how to make roasting ear bread in a 2010 interview: "You get your corn before it gets too hard, cut it off the cob, and you bake it like cornbread." It can be made in a pan, iron skillet, or baked or boiled in corn shucks.

Sweet corn with green peppers. Photo by the author.

Masa or Cornmeal is often added to other foods. It is used as a thickener in soups, stews, and combined with meat stock to make a variety of gravies. Some families made a version of atole with parched cornmeal. In a 1983 interview, Ed Procell asked, "You know what we'd do when we'd run out of coffee? Use corn. Parch corn and make coffee with that." This heavily parched "corn coffee" was sometimes called *kafioshi*.[17]

Most families ground corn with grinding stones. Some families did not have money for *metates* and/ or continued their Choctaw tradition of pounding corn in log mortars. Jim Toby said his family ground corn "in a hollowed out log with a club" and only used flour on special occasions.[18]

Roastin' Ear Bread
by Marjorie Rivers, Noble, LA, reprinted from Anoli

12 ears of corn (ground) [Cooked and cut off cob]
Salt to taste
½ cup sugar
½ cup oil
1 cup self rising flour
Grease pan or spray with Pam

Mix corn, salt, sugar, oil and flour together. Put in pan and cook at 400 degrees about 30 minutes or until golden brown.

Hotwater Cornbread by Joanne Beebe Sepeda. Photo by the author.

Roastin' Ear Bread
by Joanne Sepeda

6-8 ears fresh corn, shucked and de-silked
Oil
Salt

Cut corn off cob
Grind corn in handmill or food processor to semi-soupy consistency

If corn is milky, use as is.
If dry, add up to ¼ cup of milk
Add salt
Add 2 tbsp oil

Cover bottom of large iron skillet with oil (at least 1/8 cup)
Put skillet in oven to heat skillet & oil

Pour corn mixture into skillet
Bake at 350 until brown on edges and on top
Remove from oven, let cool for at least one hour

Shuck Bread
by Arlene V. Rivers Wright, Ebarb, LA

2 cups cornmeal (yellow or white)
1 tsp. salt
1 tsp. soda
Corn shucks (boil before using)

Mix cornmeal, soda, and salt with enough boiling water to make a very thick paste. Wrap in corn shucks like tamale and tie. Drop into deep pot of boiling water. Cover and cook for 40 minutes (or steam just like tamales until they are done).

Hot Water Cornbread by Marjorie Rivers
Noble, LA, reprinted from Anoli

4 cups self-rising yellow meal
Boiling water

Mix meal with enough boiling water so the mixture is not soupy. Put in greased pan and cook at 400 degrees for about 40 minutes or until brown.

Hot Water Cornbread
by Joanne Beebe Sepeda

1 ½ cups plain cornmeal (white or yellow)
Tsp salt
3 cups water
Bowl of cold water
Cup oil

Bring 3 cups water to a boil, pour into meal, a little at a time, stirring until well-mixed and firm (not soupy). Let sit for about 5 minutes.

Dip hands into bowl of cold water. Pat heaping Tbsp of cornmeal into a patty, place on plate. Repeat until all cornmeal is made into patties.

Bring oil in skillet to medium temperature. Add patty to hot oil. Brown on both sides. Drain.

Cornmeal Dumplings
by Joanne Beebe Sepeda

¾ cup yellow or white cornmeal
½ tsp salt
Cup of boiling water

Add cornmeal and salt to boiling water, stirring until mixture is cooked to firm consistency. Shape tablespoonfuls of mixture. These dumplings go well with any kind of cooked greens.

Corn Bread Dressing
by Elsie Parrie McLendon reprinted from Anoli

Preparation Ingredients:
1 cup chopped bell pepper
1 cup chopped celery
1 cup chopped onions
½ cup (1 stick) margarine or butter
1 pan cornbread, cooked and crumbled
1 cup chicken broth
6 boiled eggs- chopped
2 teaspoons poultry seasoning
1 to 1 ½ teaspoons ground sage
1/8 teaspoon black pepper
¼ teaspoon salt or to taste

Heat oven to 350F. Sauté celery, bell pepper, and onions in butter (or margarine) until tender. Combine mixture and remaining ingredients. Pour over crumbled cornbread and toss until bread is thoroughly moistened. Place in 8-inch square baking dish or 1 ½ quart casserole dish. Bake 40-45 minutes or until heated through.

You may also stuff dressing into a 12-pound turkey. Roast according to standard roasting directions

T A M A L E S

Tamales

"I entered the house of the Indian chief who received me benevolently , and on the instant that he learned of my need promptly brought a jar of *atole* and *tamales*…" – Athanase de Mézières in Bolton, Vol II p. 76

The most famous corn food in the area is the tamale, so it deserves its own category here. The word tamale comes from Nahuatl word *tamalii*, and the Aztecs made more than forty types of them. But corn meal wrapped in corn husks (shuckbreads), with various fillings, were common across the Americas at the time of first European contact. Tamales were first documented by the Spanish Friar Bernardo de Sahagún in the early 16th-century Mexico. Similar shuck breads were also documented by English explorer John Smith in Virginia as early as 1612.[19]

Most tribes of the Southwest United States call the food tamale,[20] but the Choctaw have *banaha*, which is made of cornmeal rather than masa. *Banaha* usually includes peas or beans mixed into the dough. As the above quote indicates, colonial sources documented tamales among Caddo peoples over 200 years ago, but the Caddo Nation of Oklahoma seems to have lost that tradition.

Tamales by Dick Sepulvado and Dorothy Remedies Harper. Photo by the author.

In Ebarb and surrounding communities, tamales were primarily made with hog's head meat. In the old days, the first step in the process was to kill a hog during the fall or winter of the year and process the meat. As Mrs. Gauthier explains:

Ruby Remedies Parrie.
Photo courtesy of Cody Bruce.

Good tamales take several days to make. The first part of the process, or day one, is making the dough using the previous instructions. On day two, my mom used fresh pork meat as filling for her tamales. We always butchered hogs so she had an abundance of pork. When Dad killed a hog, she would use the head for the meat. Cleaning a hog head took hours. Mom would wash it really good and take all the hair off with a straight razor she kept just for cleaning the heads. Then it was trimmed, taking off the ears, cutting it in half, cutting out the tongue, removing the brain, and any parts or pieces that could not be cleaned. The halves were placed in a large pot and boiled until cooked. The meat was cooled and ground into chunks. The ground meat was placed in a large pot and seasoned with salt, black pepper, parched ground cayenne, and lots of garlic. This meat was placed in the refrigerator overnight to cool. Day three was spent making the tamales. Lots of water was kept boiling on the stove top. This water was used to clean corn shuck, mix the dough, and for dipping fingers to dab tamales. Dabbing tamales is rarely seen. Mom would put a ball of dough in the center of the top of the corn shuck, the shuck was cradled in both hands and using her thumbs the dough was spread down the center of the shuck.

Nowadays, tamales are often made with pork roast (arm, shoulder, loin, rump or other cuts) purchased in the store. The other ingredients (hot pepper and/or crushed red pepper, garlic, salt and pepper, and shucks for wrapping tamales) are all commercially available.

While Mexican-style pre-made *masa* is now available in grocery stores throughout the United States, most tamale makers in the community prefer to make their own dough. In times past, the dried field corn was boiled in a large cast iron pot with oak ashes to remove the skin from the kernels. Today this hominy-making stage in the process is usually done by boiling the dry corn with commercially-available pickling lime in either the old cast iron or a new stainless steel pot.

In times past, people also made tamales with chicken. A.J. Remedies reported that mild chicken tamales were a favorite food for sick people. Some families also reported using guinea fowl, turkey, venison, beans or peas in their tamales. A few families also cooked tamales with no filling at all, nearly identical to cornmeal "shuck bread" but made with *masa*. One informant called these no-filling tamales "blanks."[21]

Dick Sepulvado making tamales, 2011. Photo by the author.

Tony Remedies, Valerie and Kim Weber, corn field, early to mid 1970s. Photo courtesy of Delores Weber.

Tamale Recipes

CAUTION: When making hominy or tamale dough, be sure to use dry field corn, NOT seed corn, which is commonly treated with highly poisonous fungicides. Boil corn and lime mixture in a stainless steel, cast iron, or Corningware pot. DO NOT use an aluminum pot because it will corrode and contaminate the corn.

Tamales
by Rhonda Remedies Gauthier

Meat:
5-10 lbs. fresh pork or hog head
2 garlic bulbs
Salt
Black Pepper
Oven parched red cayenne pepper

Masa:
Hard wood ash or commercial lye
Gallon shelled yellow dent corn
Salt
2 lb box or bucket of pure lard

Tamales ready for cooking. Photo by the author.

Fill a large cast iron pot (some ladies use a 40-gallon caldron) with water. Build a fire around the pot and bring water to a rolling boil. If using white oak ash, pour in about a ½ gallon bucket of ash. If using commercial lye, use two quarts.

Bring water back to a rolling boil and pour in 1 gallon shelled corn. If liquid begins to boil over, use a shovel to pull back hot coals from the pot. Boil the corn constantly stirring with a long wooden spoon or some type of stick to prevent sticking the corn to the bottom of the pot. Constantly moving the kernels around in the boiling liquid helps the corn to cook all at once. When corn kernels can be pierced with your fingernail and the husks start falling away from the kernels it is done. 1-2 hours cooking time, depending on the variety of corn. Dip the hominy from the hot liquid to another container filled with cold water. You will need to keep moving to several different containers filled with cold water until it is cool enough for you to wash with your hands. This will also help remove the excess husk material. Continue to wash until water is clear. Cool and grind. This process can also be done inside with corn cooked in a stainless steel pot. Make sure space is well ventilated.

An alternative to this procedure is to purchase two to four gallon cans of store bought hominy.

In a large dishpan or mixing bowl add 2 gallons of ground hominy and sprinkle in salt (to taste) and add half the lard. Boil the saved broth from cooking the meat chunks (can substitute box broth). Pour over lard and ground corn stir and mix until it begins to get soft and thick. Dough or masa should be a little soft enough to spread over shuck and you can tell if you have enough lard in the dough if it spreads even and is not sticky.

If using a hog head, make sure it is thoroughly clean. Wash it really good and remove hair that may have been left on it. Trim off any pieces where hair can't be removed. Cut off the ears, cut it in half, cut out the tongue, remove the brain, and any parts or pieces that can't be cleaned. Place the halves in large pot and boil until cooked. After the meat is cooled grind it into chunks. Place the ground meat in a large pot and season with salt, black pepper, parched ground cayenne, and lots of chopped garlic. Cook until seasonings are thoroughly absorbed into meat and refrigerate overnight to cool. If using fresh ground pork, beef or any other meat from the market skip the first steps. Season and cook meat. Let cool overnight. Lots of boiling water is needed so keep it going on the stove top. This water is used to clean corn shuck, mix the dough, and dipping fingers to dab tamales. Place a ball of dough in the center of the top of the corn shuck— the shuck is cradled in both hands— using your thumbs spread the dough down the center of the shuck. You can use spoons, machines, or a press to spread dough down the center of the shuck. Make several dozen and stack to the side. Using a spoon fill and roll the tamales.

According to Rhonda, the only difference in this recipe and Ruby Parrie's recipe is that Miss Ruby boiled her peppers, ground them and added them to the meat mix along with the pepper juice. Rhonda reports that this creates a different fragrance and different taste.

BEANS & VEGETABLES

Beans and Vegetables

Beans and Peas

Blackeyed peas, purple hull peas, pinto beans, and butter beans are favorites in the community. People eat them cooked fresh in season or dried. Rhonda Remedies Gauthier notes that depending on the size of the harvested pea and bean crop, peas and beans are preserved by drying or freezing. The beans are often flavored with pieces of meat (bacon, fat back, sausage, or neckbones).

In the past, they were dried, and, if available, jars were used for canning. The crop would be picked from the field and shelled or thrashed to separate the peas and beans from the shell. Shells were used as fodder for the farm animals.

Crowder peas, Vickie Holbrook. Photo by the author.

Beans and peas continue to be a standard daily food and are prepared and appear on the dining table as regularly as cornbread. Many elders call all sorts of beans and peas "*frijoles.*" Beans and peas are most always cooked with some type of pork meat for seasoning. They are also used in soups as fillers for extending foods for a large family. Peas are preserved by freezing, drying and saving in jars, and canning them in jars. A favorite pea is simmered purple hull peas. Gauthier relays that her mom and Momo (grandmother) would simmer some pork bacon with onions and add fresh shelled peas to the mix:

Salt and pepper was added to the mix and they would be served over steamed rice or with a meat dish and sometimes a side of turnip greens. The greens would be steamed with some fat or just salt and pepper with a dash of parched red cayenne. Pinto beans, butter beans, and limas were all cooked pretty much with this same recipe and each dish would taste a little different because of the variety of bean or pea used. A pinto bean is one that can be used in many recipes. Many people think dry beans take at least two to three hours to cook but my grandmother taught me how to cook dry pintos in less time. I thought it was the even heat from her cast iron pot, but I have cooked pintos in various types of pots and using this recipe takes less than two hours and is simple and good.

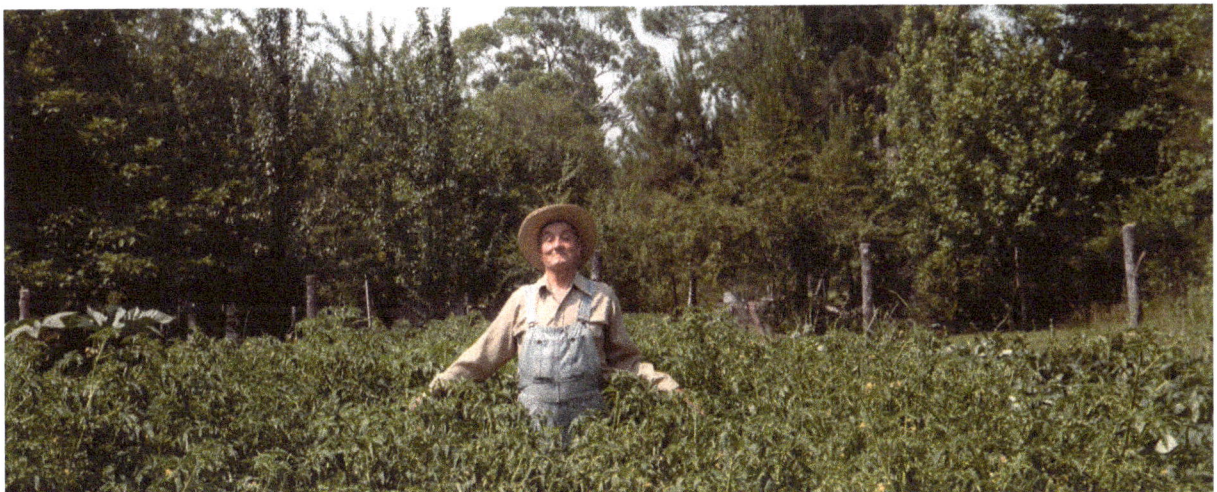

Ed Procell in his tomato patch, early 1980s. Ebarb Community Collection, CGHRC.

Dried Pintos Made Simple
by Rhonda Remedies Gauthier

1 lb. dry pintos washed in warm water and set aside
1tsp baking soda
1tsp sugar
1 med. yellow onion
Approximately 4-6 green onions chopped
1tsp paprika
4-5 c. water boiled in a 4 qrt. pot
Salt water to taste
2 T oil

Edna Procell Ezernack shelling purple hull peas, early 1980s. Ebarb Community Collection, CGHRC.

Beans are added to water along with oil, baking soda, sugar, paprika, and yellow and green onions. Add salt to taste. Cover and simmer until beans are just getting soft and remove lid. Let simmer until juice in the beans begins to thicken and beans are soft. You have beans in less than two hours.

Squash, Melons, and Pumpkin

Green and yellow summer squash varieties were and still are used fresh from the garden. Today, many freeze sliced squash for later use. This squash can be eaten raw in a salad, simmered in a skillet seasoned with onions and bacon bits, fried, or as many community members prefer, in casseroles. The flower blossoms of squash can also be eaten. Some people prefer them lightly fried. Certain varieties of squash can be eaten young as summer squash or left in the field to grow large and used for winter soups or breads, like winter squashes. When fully mature, the seeds can be removed for next season or toasted.

Watermelons are a favorite summertime food, and some people make watermelon rind jelly. Pumpkins can be made into baked or fried pies, breads, or simply sliced, cleaned, and roasted.

Gourds, an inedible crop related to squash, were grown for multiple uses. Bottle gourds might be used to hold salt or liquids. Gourds were also used as water dippers. Longnecked gourds were often used to help stuff meat into sausage casings.

Kenneth Garcie canning. Photo by the author.

Tomatoes, Okra, and Cucumbers

Tomatoes are key ingredients in salads, soups, and often included in pepper and other sauces. They can be sliced and eaten plain or with a little salt. Ripe tomatoes are also stewed or canned, and cooked with okra. Some families bread and fry green tomatoes.

Okra is usually stewed or fried. Okra with tomatoes can be frozen or canned. Cucumbers, green tomatoes, and okra can also be pickled in vinegar.

PEPPER

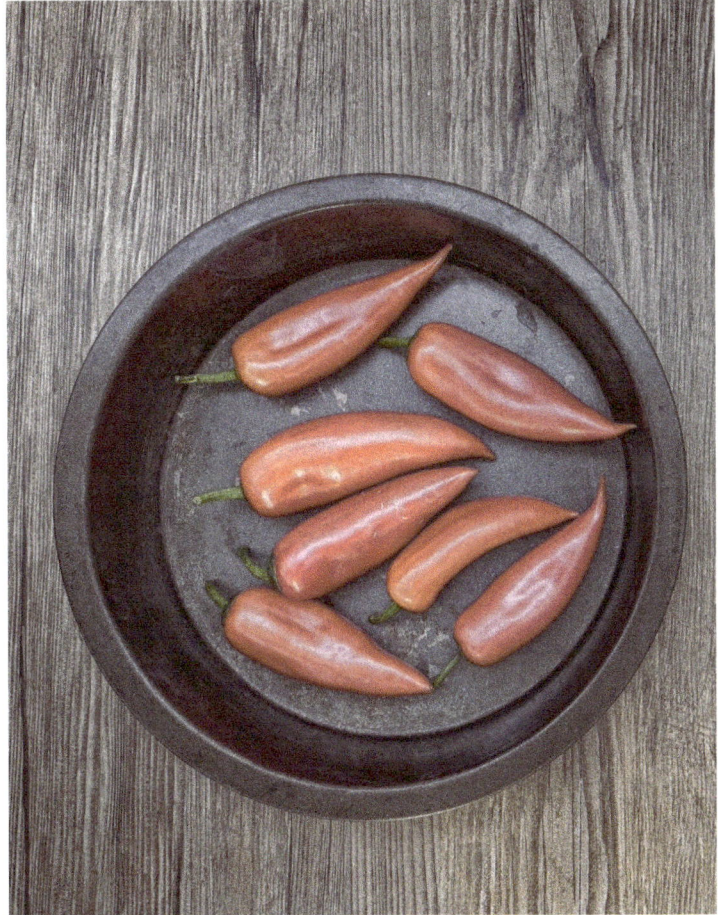

FOODS

Pepper Foods

Pepper is both the name of a range of food dishes (sometimes called pepper sauce, pepper gravy or pepper and eggs) as well as a key ingredient or important spice in other foods within the Choctaw-Apache community. Cayenne and other hot peppers are used as an appetizer, side dish, and condiment. Many Choctaw-Apache families continue to make pepper dishes, and every family has its own favorite recipe. Some families use garlic, others do not. Some cooks insist on bacon grease, while others use cooking oil or no oil at all. Unlike the tamale, this food has not enjoyed widespread commercial appeal and is nearly unknown to outsiders.

The tribe's strong pepper tradition is evidence of the influence of the "Southwest" and is provides one instance in which Choctaw-Apache food traditions are in stark contrast to the tribes of the "Southeast."

As late as the 1980s, almost every garden had plenty of pepper and one could see pepper drying on tin roofs or braided on porches or hung in kitchens to dry. Freezers have superseded drying and canning as methods of preserving pepper now, and freezers allow families to enjoy garden-grown "green" peppers year-round. Pepper imports from California and Mexico now readily available in stores means less pepper is grown in gardens.

The food was traditionally used as a medicine as well. Peppers are high in Vitamin C and, purportedly, good for circulation, joints and arthritis.

Dried peppers. Photo by the author.

Homemade Pepper
by Kenneth Garcie, Ebarb, LA

"…The way my moma made it and the way my papa liked it, with plenty of garlic. We never measure any of it. Just pick the pepper fresh from the garden, about a half gallon full. (Maybe an apron full when my Moma went into the garden.) Stem and bring to a boil. Grind on the *metate* or in a mill when cool enough. Prepare cooking pot by frying two or three pieces of bacon or fat back with a hand full of garlic ground up in the metate or chopped. Do not burn garlic. Add ground up pepper and cook for three or four minutes. Add tomatoes fresh if possible or canned if not. This cools the hot down. Cook for ten or fifteen minutes then add eggs to further cool the hot. Add salt to taste. Continue to cook ten to twenty minutes." Kenneth says that his pepper is really good with a pan of hot biscuits fresh from the oven.

Pepper (and mill gravy) soup. Photo by the author.

Homemade Pepper
by Kimberly Procell, Noble, LA, reprinted from Anoli

3 tablespoons ground pepper
½ onion- diced
2 garlic cloves
1 can Rotel tomatoes (mild or hot)
2 eggs
Season to taste

Combine the first four ingredients. Let simmer for 15 minutes. Add eggs. Cook another 10-15 minutes.

Pepper
by Margie Procell, Zwolle, LA, reprinted from Anoli

2 cups ground tomatoes
2 cups ground green pepper
¼ cup oil
2 beaten eggs
Salt, black pepper, and garlic to taste

Simmer tomatoes, oil, black pepper, and garlic until thickened (about 20 minutes). Add pepper and simmer (another 20 minutes). Then add eggs and cook until eggs are done. Serve with anything you wish.

Red pepper can be used as a condiment or a side dish. Photo by the author.

Quick Pepper
by Joanne Sepeda

1 pint jar of diced, canned hot green pepper
Water
Garlic powder
2 eggs
Tbsp oil

Add canned pepper, ¼ cup water, garlic powder and 1 tbsp oil. Bring to boil on medium heat for about 10 minutes. Break 2 eggs and scramble in mixture. Cook until eggs are done.

"Shalasa" – Pepper Dish
by Kimberly Procell, Noble, LA, reprinted from Anoli

1 pound hamburger meat or pound of steak
7 chili peppers (green or red)
1 onion- diced
1 tsp. garlic salt
1 tsp. garlic powder
1 tsp. salt
2 cans Rotel tomatoes (hot or mild)

Cook all ingredients together for 45 minutes or until done.

Pepper Gravy
by Rhonda Remedies Gauthier

1 qrt of ground green jalapeños
½ medium onion chopped
2 garlic cloves chopped
2 eggs
2 fresh tomatoes (remove skin) chopped
Salt
Bacon, about 4 pieces chopped

Render bacon in deep skillet or 2 quart pot. Add onions, garlic, and salt. Cook until onions glaze then add the ground pepper and a small amount of water. Simmer for about 15 minutes and add tomatoes. Tomatoes are optional. Cook for another few minutes and add eggs one at a time constantly stirring. When eggs are completely blended into mix simmer for about 5 minutes and serve.

Kenneth Garcie's spicy red pepper.
Photo by the author.

Green pepper by Martha Parrie Etheridge.
Photo by the author.

Biscuits.
Photo by the author.

FRY BREADS

Frybreads

Frybread is a Native American food common throughout the United States and varies from region to region. Many people assume that frybread came about from commodity disbursement on western reservations in the late 1800s, but the tradition is much older. Frybread is actually product of early frontier cultural interaction.

People in the community historically had two names for frybread: *clepes* and *chudisgetchies*. Either type of frybread might be cooked in a frypan, or on a griddle with oil, or in more recent times, deep fried in an iron skillet. *Clepe* comes from the French word crêpe. *Chudisgetchies* (also chudisketchies, chirriaskedies or chirrisquetes) might be related to the obscure verb *chirriar*, a Spanish word that means "to hiss, creek, or squeek;" the sound the frybread makes when it hits the grease. The word more likely comes from *chigustei*, an Apache word that is used for flatbreads made from wheat flour, and literally translates as "cooked on embers." By the late 20th-century, most families used either *clepes* or *chudisgeties* to describe all types frybreads, but some families continued to use both terms and distinguish differences between frybread types.

In the late 20th-century, members of the community began attending powwows and intertribal events and were happy to find the familiar comfort food there. It was just like the *clepes* my mom used to make," one elder recalled. As the unique local 18th-century Spanish trade language in the area has been replaced with English, people began referring to all varieties of this food as "frybread." *Clepes* and chudisgeties used to be eaten plain, with cane syrup or with honey. Nowadays, frybread is just as often eaten with powdered sugar or as part of an "Indian taco."

Frybread cooking in a cast iron pot. Photo by the author.

Fry Bread
by Arlene V. Rivers Wright, Ebarb, LA

5 cups self-rising flour
½ cup oil
Sweet milk, amount to make biscuit dough

Mix flour, oil, and lukewarm milk. Let dough stand and rise about one hour. Roll the dough on a board and cut to shape desired. Fry the bread in skillet using oil for frying.

Fry Bread
by Rhonda Remedies Gauthier

4 c plain flour
½ tsp salt
1 tsp baking soda
2 Tbsp oil
Water

Mix all ingredients. Add water until mix is almost soft and pliable (like pizza dough). Using dry flour rub on hands and work dough into a 4-inch flat bread cake and drop into a hot shallow skillet of oil. Oil does not need to cover dough. When dough browns turn it over to brown other side. The process takes about two to three minutes on each side. Continue these steps until all dough is used. Store bread in a deep bowl and cover with a towel. Good served with syrup, jelly, or for making Indian Tacos.

Frybread
by Gayla Beebe Rivers

Mrs. Rivers explained that her grandmother, Annie Garcie Beebe, used to make what she called "Cowboy Bread, "a small but thick type of frybead."

2 cups self-rising flour
Add water until flour pulls away from sides of
 bowl
Oil

Sprinkle flour on wax paper. Work flour in bowl, pinch off size of ½ cup, pat in hands or on wax paper. Drop into hot oil, cook until golden brown.

Frybread by Gayla Rivers. Photo by the author.

F R U I T S

B E R R I E S

N U T S

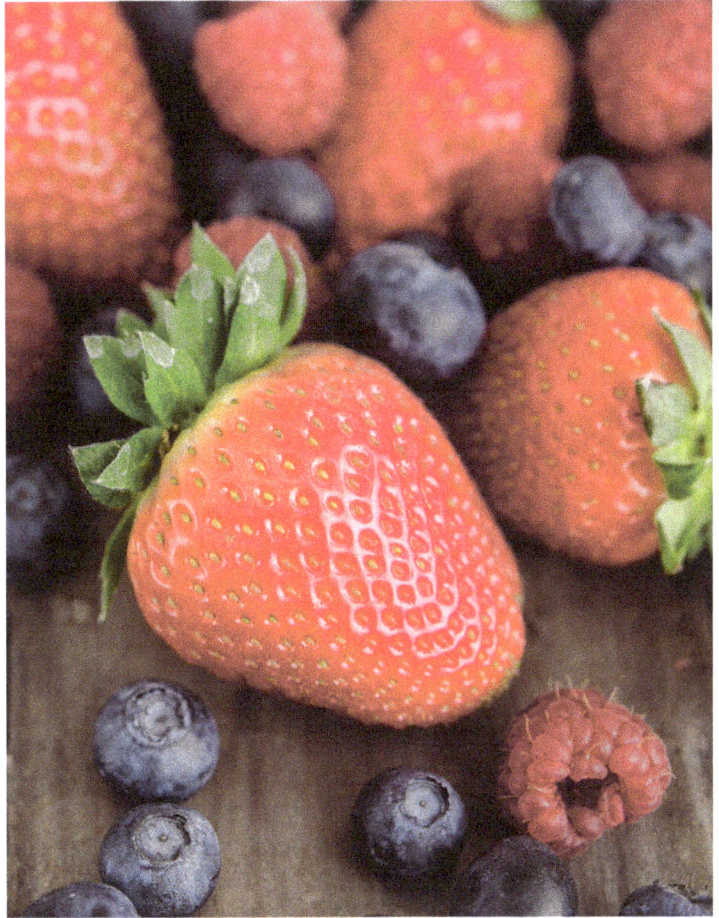

Fruits, Berries, and Nuts

Wild fruit and berries can be eaten raw as a snack, made into jams and jellies, or desserts like berry dumplings. Berry dumplings are most often made blueberries, huckleberries (wild blueberries), blackberries and dewberries. All of these berries are native to North America and are common in western Sabine parish, and tribal members gather them annually during the late spring and early summer.

Mayhaw and muscadine are still favorite wild fruits for making jelly. Mayhaws are found under hardwoods along lakes, creek "branches" and in bottom land. They are harvested beginning in early spring. Muscadines ripen at the end of summer. Pecans are gathered in the fall and eaten raw, or used in cookies, candies, and pies.

Johnny Lee Rivers gathers wild plums, 2014. Photo by author.

Older community members also remember eating wild "fox grapes" and "possum grapes," as well as wild persimmons, blackhaw (*negritos*), "wild bananas" (pawpaw) and chinkapin (chinquapin) nuts. Today's pine forest plantations are far less diverse than the mixed hardwood and pine forests of the past, and many of these cultivars (including the chinkapin) are now exceedingly rare in the area.

Figs, pears, peaches, all "old world" domesticates, have been grown for hundreds of years by Choctaw-Apache ancestors. Peach trees, originally from Asia, were brought by Europeans and spread quickly among indigenous people. They are still grown in the community.

Blackberry Dumplings
by Rhonda Remedies Gauthier

4-quart pot
4 cups of berries thoroughly washed
1 ½ cups of sugar
4 cups of plain flour
1 tsp. of salt
2 Tbsp. baking powder
1 stick of butter
4 table spoons of water

Place berries in pot. Add enough water to cover, add sugar and simmer. While berries are simmering make dumplings. Place sifted flour in a large bowl, add all dry ingredients, salt and baking powder. Make a hole in the center of flour and add butter. Using a fork, mash the butter into the flour while adding water one tablespoon at a time. Mix until flour forms a ball. Pour mix out onto a floured surface and using a rolling pin flatten dough to about a quarter inch. Cut small squares and drop one at a time into berry mix. Make sure the berry mix is heated to a low boil. Add dumplings until juice gets slightly thick, and simmer until dumplings are cooked.

Leatha Rivers's Peach Cobbler
by Cody Bruce

Leatha Leone was born to Patrick Leone and Lucila "Lucy" Sepulvado in 1917. She married Jacob Lee Roy "Jake" Rivers in 1937 and passed away in 2011.

To prepare: Preheat oven to 325 degrees.
Ingredients:
1 cup sugar
1 cup self-rising four
1 cup milk
1 egg
1 Tbsp. vanilla
1 stick butter
1 large can of peaches (draining is optional)
[can substitute frozen or fresh]

Directions:
Melt one stick of butter in 9 X 13" baking pan. Combine sugar, flour, milk, egg, and vanilla. Mix until batter is smooth then pour batter over melted butter. Drop peaches around in pan over batter. Place in oven and bake for 35-45 minutes or until edges are golden brow. Serve with homemade vanilla ice cream.

Canning Peaches
by Rhonda Remedies Gauthier

Wash jars, lids and rings. Let them set in hot water until needed.

Wash and peel five quarts of peaches. Cut the peaches into quarters. Measure six cups of peaches into a large pot. Add four cups of sugar to the peaches. Simmer over medium heat until sugar melts. If you do not have enough liquid in the pot, add enough liquid to just cover the peaches. Cook for about ten minutes and add Sure-Jell. Simmer about fifteen minutes. Add fruit to jars and top with lids and rings. Do not tighten the lids all the way. Place jars of fruit in a large canning pot. Add enough water to just cover the jars. Let the water come to a boil and boil for ten to twenty minutes. Turn off the heat and remove jars of fruit with tongs. Using a towel, tighten the lids by hand and let cool. As the jars cool the lids will pop and seal.

Most any fruit (strawberries, blackberries etc.) can be canned this way.

If you just want to can apples and pears without use for making pies later. Just cook the fruit with a small amount of sugar and cook in water until tender. Or place the fruit in large mouth jars, add just enough sugar to sweeten water you add to cover fruit. Close with lids and rings, place in a large pot, cover with water and boil for about twenty minutes.

Fried Pies
by Rhonda Remedies Gauthier

Use same crust recipe as for pies.
Sweet potato pie
4-5 sweet potatoes
1 c sugar
½ stick of butter
1 tsp vanilla

Cube sweet potatoes and place in a large pot to boil. Cut until tender and mash. Add sugar, cinnamon and vanilla. In a large deep fryer heat oil while preparing pies. Roll out dough and cut rounds with a small bowl. You can make half-moon shaped pies or 4" rounds. Fill and crimp the edges to seal. Using a spatula, drop pies into hot oil and let one side brown and then turn to brown the other side.

Peach pies
by Rhonda Remedies Gauthier

4-5 peaches
1 c sugar
½ tsp allspice
1 tsp cornstarch or flour

Wash, peel and slice peaches. Cook peaches with sugar until tender. Add cornstarch, let thicken, and add allspice. Using same instructions as with sweet potato pies, fill shell and fry.

FOOD & FAMILY

OLD TIME

CULTURAL CHANGE & CONTINUITY

Food and Family

Food is often synonymous with family. Families pass down food traditions through the generations, providing forms of cultural continuity. Most of the foods in this book are present at the numerous Choctaw-Apache family reunions in Sabine Parish each year.

Plate at the Remedies-Ezernack-Parrie Family Reunion, 2011. Photo by the author.

Author's plate, George and Susan Remedies Family Reunion. Photo by the author.

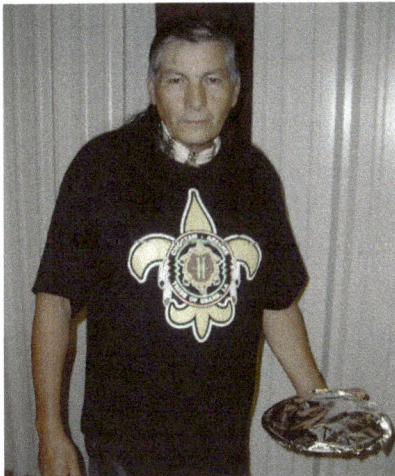

Daniel Parrie, 2011. Photo by the author.

George and Susan Remedies family reunion, 2011. Photo by the author.

Chicken and Dumplings
by Marjorie Rivers, Noble, LA, reprinted from Anoli

1 whole chicken	¼ cup oil	3 cloves of garlic (chopped finely)
Salt and black pepper to taste	Water	

Simmer garlic in oil until it gets soft. Then add chicken, black pepper and salt. Cook on high heat ten minutes, stirring occasionally. Then add enough boiling water to cover the chicken. Let cook about 30 minutes. Then add dumplings.

Dumplings   4 cups of self-rising flour

Add cold water to make the dough thick enough to roll out. Roll out and cut into strips about 2 in. wide. Let one layer at a time cook until all dough is gone. As each layer cooks stir into the chicken.

Zeatha Rivers's Chicken and Dumplings
by Cody Bruce

1 hen
1 ½ teaspoons black pepper
1 teaspoon salt
3 cups all-purpose flour
1 cup water (chilled)

Add to taste:
Red pepper
Onion powder
Garlic powder

1. Rinse chicken and place in a large cooking pot. Cover chicken with water. Add black pepper and salt. Bring to a boil and cook until chicken is tender.

2. After chicken is cooked, strain broth and remove skin. Debone chicken if desired. Return deboned chicken and strained broth to chicken pot.

3. In a large mixing bowl, combine flour and water. Stir until soft dough is formed. Knead dough on floured surface until firm.

4. Roll and pat dough to about 1/8" thickness, cut into ½" or 1" strips.

5. Bring chicken and broth to boil. Drop in dumplings one at a time, stirring only lightly when dropping dumplings to prevent dumplings from sticking together.

6. When all dough is in broth, reduce heat and simmer until dough is firm, about 10 minutes.

Serve with cornbread.

Juanna Janie Toby Remedies in the Kitchen. Photo courtesy of Cody Bruce.

Leatha Leone Rivers making Chicken and Dumplings. Photo courtesy of Cody Bruce.

Old Time

"We raised everything. We didn't have much money. Didn't need much…We smoked our own bacon, we dried our own beef [and] pickled our own beef… We dried our own beef jerky…" – Jim Toby

My great-grandfather George Remedies told interviewers that "back then people didn't get sick like they do now, with heart problems and cancer." He attributed poor health to eating canned foods and a general over-reliance on store-bought foods. "We raised a lot of pumpkins, sweet potatoes. We didn't have to buy lard or any meat. There were plenty of rabbits, squirrels, and birds. All we'd buy is coffee, flour, and meal. We made all kinds of peas and beans. You'd hardly see anyone sick in those days." In addition to growing and hunting foods, most Choctaw-Apache ancestors also consumed far less refined sugar than tribal members do today. Families usually grew ribbon cane or sorghum to make syrup, and robbed beehives for wild honey.

In times past, most community members ate the brains of beef, pork, and wild game. Community members also milked cows and made their own buttermilk and butter. Hog brains can be cooked whole, in-head, when cooking the head for tamales. Another way is to split the head and remove the brains. Beef brains were often cooked with green onions and/or onions, and scrambled in a pan with eggs. According to Howard Rivers, this practice fell into disuse prior to "mad cow" scare and can be traced to the decline of families raising and butchering their own meat. Fewer families butchering their own meat and the prevailing opinions of outsiders also led to the decline of utilizing animal blood in recipes.

Simple cooking techniques used to be employed during hunting and fishing trips. Any fish with scales can be covered in mud (clay) and cooked in a fire or on coals. When it is cracked open the scales and skin will come off. According to Howard Rivers, turtle can be cooked whole in-shell on the fire. The meaty, edible parts are mostly separate from entrails.

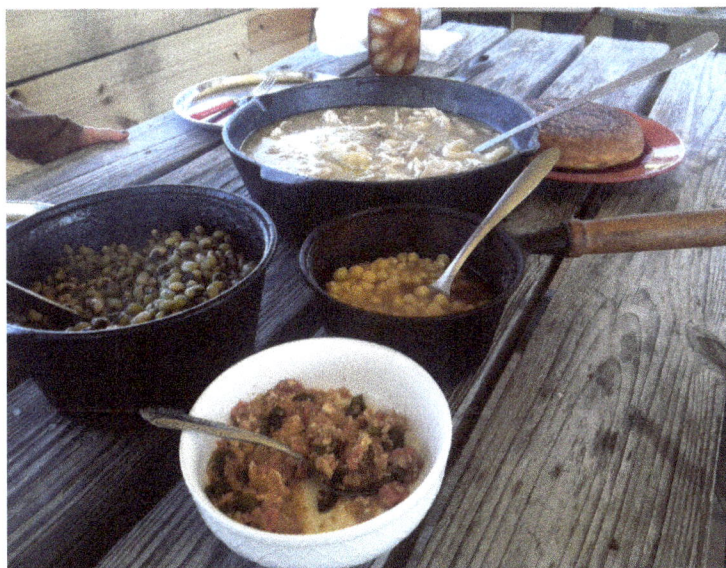

Old style cooking prepared by Johnny Lee Rivers. Chicken and dumplings, corn bread, hominy, purple hull peas, spicy pepper with iced tea. Photo by the author.

Eggs and Wild Onions
by Arlene V. Rivers Wright, Ebarb, LA

Wild onions, cut up (whatever amount you want).
1 cup shortening [or lard], melted.
1 cup water. 6 eggs.

Cut up enough wild onions to fill a 6- to 10-inch skillet. Place water, shortening and onions into skillet. Salt to taste and fry until almost all the water is gone (15 to 20 minutes). Break eggs on top of the onions and stir well. Fry until the eggs are done. Serve hot.

Pork and Hominy
by Pati Laroux, Zwolle, LA, reprinted from Anoli

2 ½ cups dry hominy
Salt and black pepper to taste
Water
Pork: neckbones, pork fingers, or pork chops (cut in pieces)

Boil hominy until tender (this takes a while). You may want to cook in crock pot. Cook pork separately. When hominy is done add pork to the same pot. Season to taste.

Squirrel and Gravy
by Rhonda Remedies Gauthier

Quarter several squirrels (days fresh kill)
salt and pepper
cover the squirrel with flour
dip quarters in cold water and flour one more time

In a large four- to five-quart pot, brown pieces in hot oil. Remove from oil and add four chopped cloves of garlic and flour. Brown flour and add water to make gravy. Return squirrel quarters to the pot and add enough water to cover squirrel. Now add the squirrel heads to the pot. Steam over medium heat until squirrel is tender and heads are floating. Serve over steamed rice or steam potatoes.

Instructions for eating the heads. The head has little or no meat on it. The brain is the treat. Place the squirrel head on a plate and take your spoon and gently tap on the head at the center of the skull cap. The bone will break and then you can use your spoon to scoop out the brain. Eat it with lots of gravy and rice.

Baked Coon
by Rhonda Remedies Gauthier

1 large coon, skinned and quartered
Ground, parched red cayenne peppers
Salt
4 large sweet potatoes
2 large sweet onions quartered
4 garlic cloves finely chopped
½ c oil

Place coon meat into a large roaster pan. Rub the meat with oil, salt, garlic, pepper and place quartered onions into the pan. Add enough water to cover the bottom of pan. Cover and place in 350' oven and cook until meat gets tender. Remove from oven and place large chunks of sweet potatoes around the meat. Place back into oven and cook until potatoes are tender and meat has browned.

Polk Salad (Poke Sallet) with eggs
by Rhonda Remedies Gauthier

Note: Polk Salad is a poisonous plant. Pick in the spring when leaves are young and tender, when the plant is less than 18" tall, and leaves are less than 6".

2-4 quart pot and deep 12-inch skillet
Polk salad leaves, thoroughly washed and torn into pieces
½ onion, 2-4 eggs, salt, ground dried red cayenne pepper

Place leaves in pot and cover with water. Bring to boil and strain. Discard the water. Recover leaves and boil again. Strain and repeat the same instructions about 4 times. Strain and place to the side and let stand. Heat oil in skillet, add chopped onions and cook, add greens to the skillet and cook about 5 minutes until greens heat through and through. Add eggs to the mix one at a time and stir. Add salt and pepper and cook until well mixed.

Cultural Change and Continuity

The culture of the Choctaw-Apache community is not static. In the 21st-century fewer and fewer people are cooking from scratch. However, some traditions continue despite technological change and traditional methods of cooking persist despite the adoption of new technologies.

One hundred fifty years ago, great-great grandmothers cooked outdoors or at an earthen hearth with a wood fire. About one hundred years ago, some of our great grandmothers shifted from cooking on an open outdoor fire or a wood hearth to wood burning stoves. In 1982, Mrs. Annie Sepulvado recalled: "…we had a little wood stove. But in the chimney, we had little skillets- little old skillet with legs like this, you know…they taste real good… that's the only way my mother cooked."

By the mid-20th-century propane burning stoves became widely available. Now people use modern gas or electric stoves and ovens. Despite all of this change, some people continue to cook remarkably similar meals to the ones their ancestors prepared.

Likewise, they went from the labor-intensive process of grinding (or pounding) corn by hand to using a factory-made hand grinder to using a food processor.

Corn was ground by hand with a *metate* (grinding stone) or pounded in a log: They just got a big rock so wide and long….We'd get these here factory-mades, some of them had legs that'd set them up on the floor. That's how we'd grind our corn until these food choppers came in…" – Edna Procell Ezernack 1982

My people used to grind corn with a hollowed out log and a club. -Jim Toby, 1982

By the middle twentieth-century, people transitioned from the *metate* to commercially-produced hand grinders to make masa. During the 1990s, masa was made from scratch with the aid of electric food processors. Despite the many changes in technology, many community members proudly continue to make corn dough (*masa*) from scratch.

Sally Sepulvado grinding lyed corn on metate, early 1980s. Ebarb Community Collection, CGHRC.

MEATS & WILD GAME

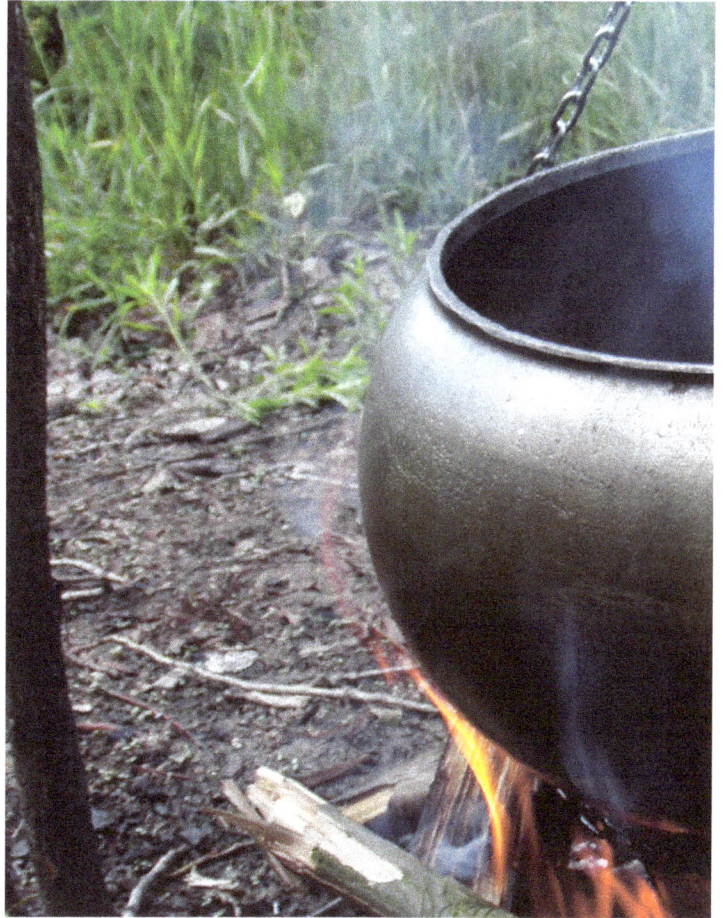

Meats and Wild Game

Meats are a big part of Choctaw-Apache culture and the tribal community has always fished and hunted wild game to supplement the food they grew. Despite most families' having had free range hogs and a couple of milk cows, many elders remember the majority of the animal protein they ate as children coming from the woods. John Procell, Johnnie Lee Rivers, and Howard Rivers all recounted hunting and fishing techniques for a variety of fish and game. Wild game is leaner (lower in fat) than beef and pork. Although most tribal members eat more store-bought pork and beef today than ever, hunting remains popular and wild foods continue to be an important part of the tribe's culture today.

Jim Toby cooking barbeque. Photo courtesy of Cody Bruce.

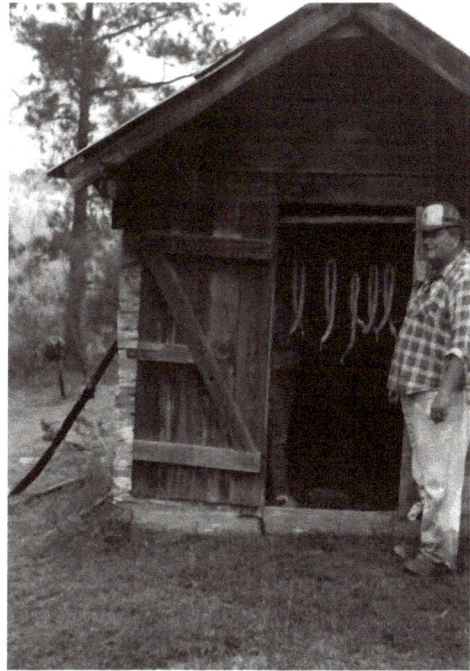

Sausage making. Elmer Procell, early 1980s. Ebarb Community Collection, CGHRC.

Crisp Salt Pork
by Arlene V. Rivers Wright, Ebarb, LA

Select salt pork with as much lean as possible, wipe off the excess salt then slice thin. Place the slices in a pan of water and bring to a boil. Pour off the water then dry with a paper towel, lay the slices in a cold frying pan and fry until crisp. This is good served with fried or scrambled eggs, also is great with beans, turnip greens, and cornbread.

Pork meatball soup (Begonas or Bogres [albóndigas])
by Martha Parrie Etheridge, Coon Ridge

Grind raw pork roast (or have it ground)
Water
garlic salt
red pepper (ground)
green onion blades

Mix ingredients together, into golf ball or smaller sized balls. Roll in flour. Add to boiling water. Boil for 5 minutes Add salt. Add a little cornmeal as thickener to soup.

Red Pepper Soup
by Martha Parrie Etheridge, Coon Ridge

Boil meat (pork neckbones or chicken)
Add crushed, dried red pepper
Boil together, add cornmeal as thickener

To make green pepper soup, boil fresh or frozen green pepper and add it instead of dried red pepper.

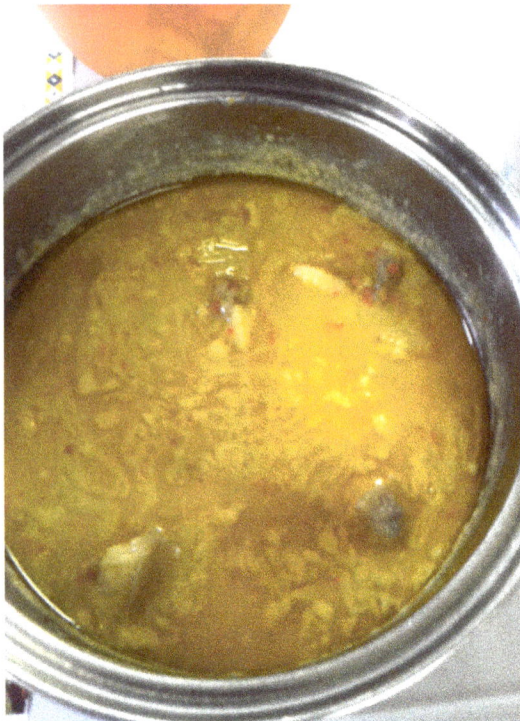

Pork meatball soup Martha Parrie Etheridge. Photo by the author.

Turtle Soup
by Howard Rivers, Zwolle, LA

Turtle is traditionally cooked in "pepper soup" with cornmeal thickener or in a kind of tomato sauce piquante. This is Howard's unique and flavorful version of the latter.

2 lbs cleaned turtle meat
Oil
Cup flour
Spices (Howard uses Tony Chachere's™ spice blend)
1 onion, 1 bell pepper, green onions, ½ stick celery cut into small pieces (can use precut seasoning mix or "fresh cuts")
(2) 8 oz cans of tomato sauce
1 can Rotel™ hot diced tomatoes with peppers
2 tbsp brown sugar

Brown turtle meat with a little oil in the bottom of a pan, lid off, cooking off excess water from turtle meat. Take turtle meat out and reserve. Add flour, making a light or medium brown gravy. Lightly saute. Add tomato sauce and Rotel ™. Add meat back in. Add water as necessary to achieve desired thickness. Add Tony's ™. Add sugar. Reduce to low heat, stir. Cook until meat is tender (varies depending on the size and age of turtle).

Turtles in bed of truck ca. 1983. Photo courtesy of Howard Rivers.

Rabbit or Squirrel
by Elsie Parrie McLendon, reprinted from Anoli

Cut rabbit or squirrel into pieces, soak overnight in salted water (one part vinegar, one part water). When ready to prepare, remove from liquid, rinse and dry. Then fry on all sides.

Preparation Ingredients:
1 quart water
2 tablespoons flour
1 minced onion
2 garlic cloves
1 bell pepper chopped
2 tomatoes
Hot pepper to taste

Brown onion in flour, add water and tomatoes. Then add remaining ingredients. Pour over rabbit or squirrel. Cover and simmer approximately one hour or until meat is tender.

Meat grilling at the 2014 Choctaw-Apache Powwow. Photo by the author.

Elmer Procell cutting hog meat, early 1980s. Ebarb Community Collection, CGHRC.

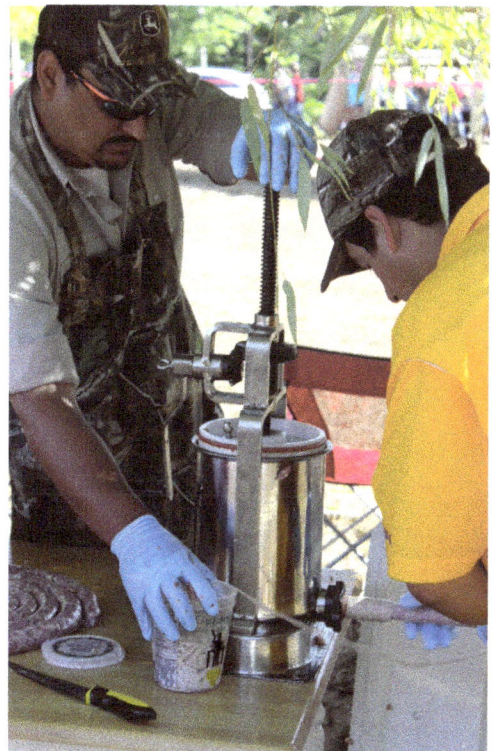

Brian Sepuvado demonstrates the art of making sausage at the 2014 Choctaw-Apache Powwow. Photo by the author.

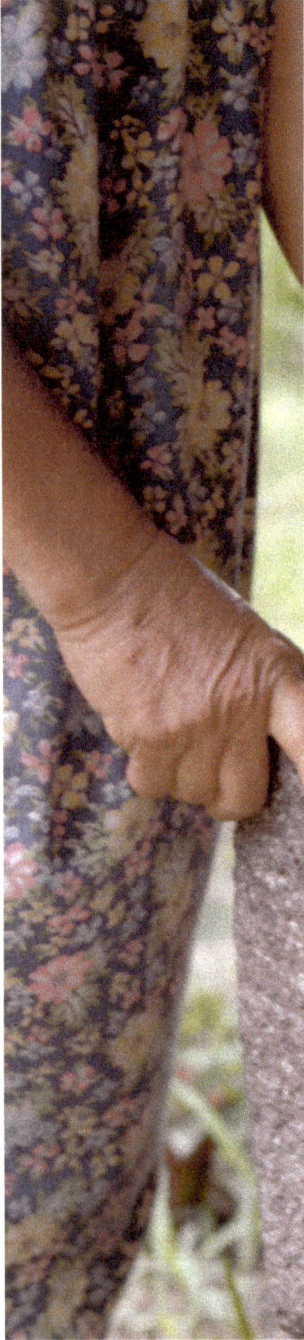

Comparative Context

While Choctaw-Apache traditional foods are distinctive, there are numerous similarities between them and traditional foods of the Choctaw, Caddo, and Cane River Creole communities. Tamales are eaten by Apache, Navajo, Cane River Creoles, as well as the peoples of Mexico.

Choctaw-Apache foods are most similar to the Choctaw and Caddo peoples. Caddo people once ate tamales but no longer. Choctaw have *banaha*, which is similar to the tamale. Caddo and Choctaw grape dumplings, and Choctaw blackberry cobbler are similar to Choctaw-Apache blackberry dumplings. Like the Choctaw-Apache, most tribes of the southeast used to eat polk salad and continue to eat at wild (green) onions and eggs.

There are other important similarities between Choctaw-Apache foods and that of other tribes. One Choctaw-Apache frybread recipe includes milk. This ingredient is somewhat unusual in Indian country, but used by the Caddo. Unfortunately, most tribes have yet to publish comprehensive foodways studies, so a more detailed comparison is arduous without additional field study.

As previously noted, the use of pepper foods in the Choctaw-Apache community is one major point of divergence from tribes of the southeast and more akin to tribes of the Southwest. The word some Choctaw-Apache elders used to describe frybread could possibly be related to *chigustei*, which the Ft. Sill Apache say means "cooked on embers," or *tsegustei*, "cooked on a rock."[22] Other "mystery words" in our lexicon might also have Southern Athabaskan (Apachean) roots. Perhaps a linguist will take interest in these words and continue specialized research along these lines. Acorn stew is also a well-known Apache food. I have been unable to identify acorn foods other than a single example of parched acorn coffee in Choctaw-Apache oral histories or living traditions.

Choctaw banaha. Photo courtesy of Devon Mihesuah.

Oklahoma-style grape dumplings are a modern adaption, usually made with Welch's grape juice. Photo courtesy of Sarah Ponca Stock (Osage Nation)

CULTURAL LOSS

CULTURAL SURVIVAL

Cultural Loss

The community has faced the assault on subsistence farming and hunting from the introduction of the railroad at Zwolle in 1898 to the destruction of old growth forests, the building of Highway 171 in the 1920s, and the end of the open free range in the 1950s brought about by the logging industry, and to the flooding of bottomlands used for hunting, fishing and farming before the Toledo Bend dam in the 1960s. The community has shifted from subsistence hunting, farming and trading in the 18th-century to mixed subsistence and agricultural wage work in the 19th-century, to wage work in the timber industry mixed with subsistence farming in the earliest part of the 20th century to what is now dependency on wage work.

One major change is the abundance of many unhealthy foods coupled with food waste. Waste was once unheard of in this community. People made careful use of their limited resources, and, like Indian people throughout the United States, had a history of making good use of virtually every part of plants and animals. Sassafras roots were used to make tea, while the wood might be used as beanpoles or for smoking meat. Leaves could be used as a flavoring or thickening agent in soups. The community had a history of hunting, growing, and raising one's own food. According to Susan Sepulvado in 1983, "We'd buy flour, sugar, coffee, rice…and the rest of the stuff, we would raise it.. [The hogs] ran wild in the woods, so we wouldn't have to feed them too much."[23]

Metate, early 1980s. Ebarb Community Collection, CGHRC.

Community members also raised hogs on scraps. According to Margie Remedies, "If the pumpkins started going bad, you gave them to the hogs. Anything that you didn't' eat, the hogs got." John Remedies said that hogs were often fed pea hulls. Edna Meshell Parrie fed her hogs watermelon rinds.[24]

Many families had strong rules against wasting food. According to Mary Remedies, "I grew up believing that wasting food was a sin. I thought it was in the Bible."[25]

Elders continue to lament cultural change and loss of traditions. Some quotes from elders in the late 20th-century summed up their concerns:

"We haven't made any [sausage] in a long time. See, we used to have a good many hogs, but now we just have one… (discussion of sugar mill, raising sugar cane and chickens)…and raising everything's done gone away. I don't guess you'll be seeing that no more- that's old time.   - Gus and Annie Sepulvado, 1982

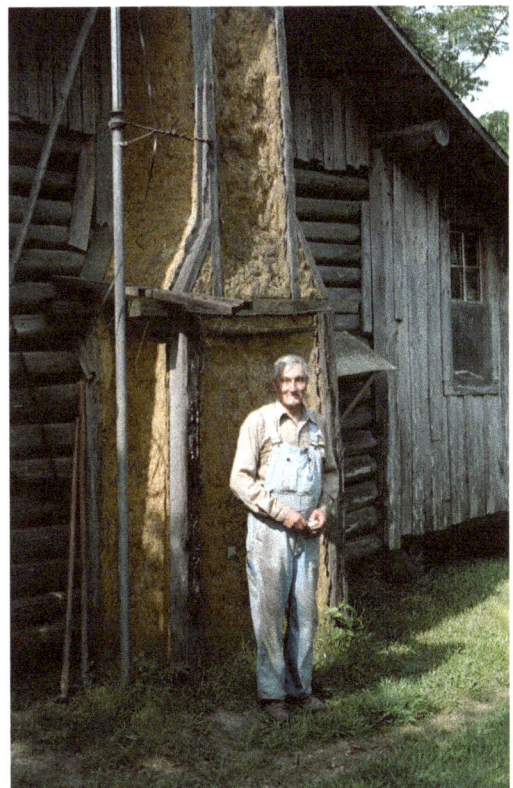

Old House with mud chimney, early 1980s. Ebarb Community Collection, CGHRC.

"I liked to listen to the old people talk. They'd tell how there used to be wildcats and the people only settled here and there in the woods….And there used to be squirrels so close you could shoot out your back porch and hit one." – Josephine Santos Paddie, 1983

"Animals aren't here anymore because people don't farm anymore and the trees don't make fruit anymore. The timber is all cut out. Some people believe that some trees are female and some are male. They have to have a pair to make fruit. The animals are all gone. Years ago you could go into the fields and scare up quail to kill or find a rabbit and coons at night."
– John Remedies 1999

Some community members still tell legends about the old people hunting bear and eating or drinking of bear fat, although the animal became largely extinct in Sabine Parish approximately one hundred years ago.

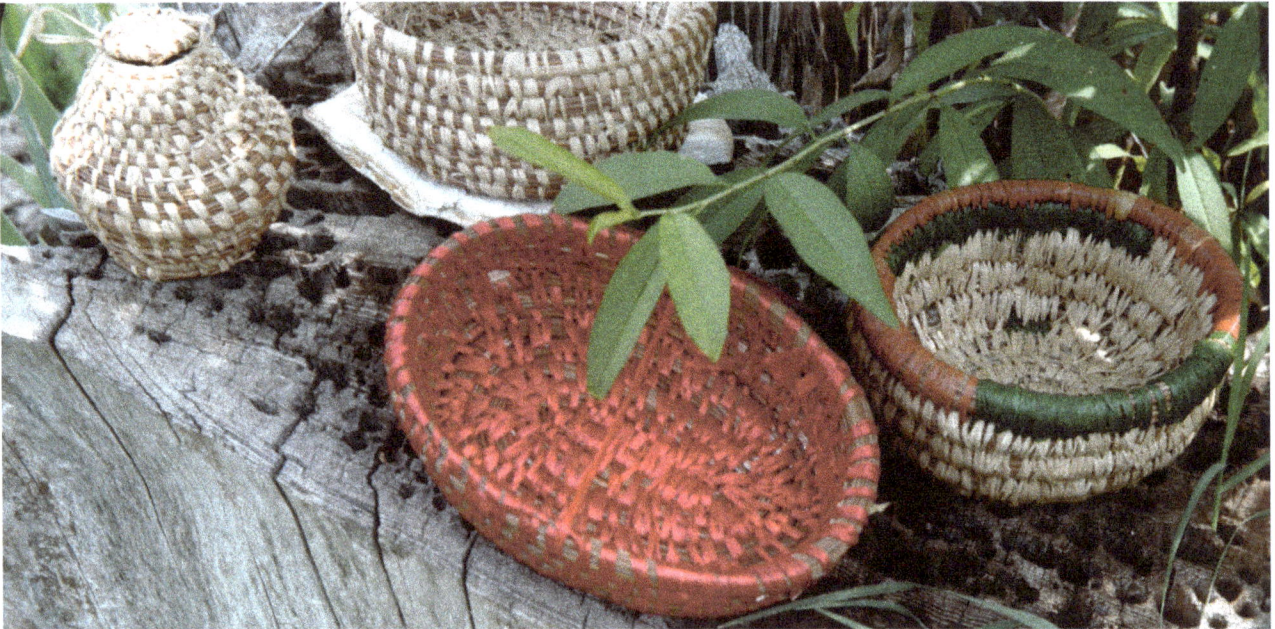

Pine needle baskets , early 1980s. Ebarb Community Collection, CGHRC.

White oak baskets, early 1980s. Ebarb Community Collection, CGHRC.

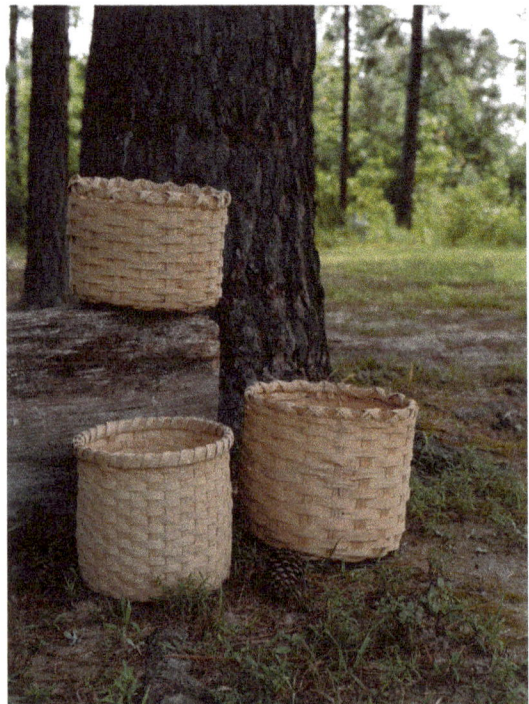

Cultural Survival

Aprerequisite for cultural survival is physical survival. For the culture to survive, first the people must survive. Culturally-appropriate healthy food choice is an important part of that survival. Secondly, a holistic view of our food traditions and contemporary food practices enables tribe to truly exercise food sovereignty.

Food as Medicine

Fresh and low-processed foods are more likely to be healthy than processed, and packaged ones. In addition, many traditional food preparation techniques add nutritional value. For example, masa is superior to ground cornmeal. It improves the availability of the corn's amino acids, greatly increases the calcium content of the corn, and increases the B-vitamin (especially Niacin) content. Some foods are used as traditional treatments to a variety of ailments. At the same time, many of the highly-processed foods our community eats today are loaded with high-fructose corn syrup and other added sugars, as well as a long list of additives. Many of our "traditional foods" —most especially those foods and cooking techniques brought across the Atlantic Ocean from Europe – are high in fat, sugar and in calories. As the old adage goes, "you are what you eat."

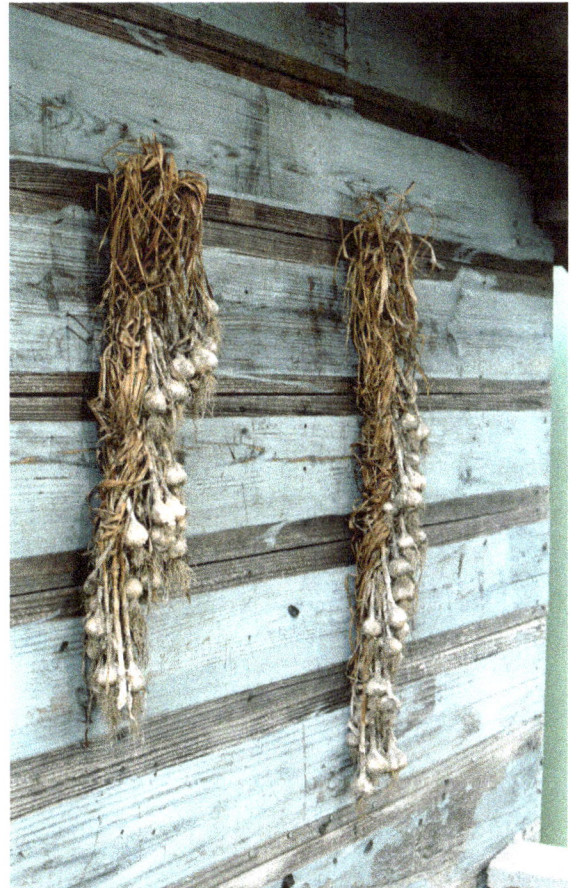

Garlic drying, early 1980s. Ebarb Community Collection, CGHRC.

Health and Food Choice

The community is one beset with diabetes, obesity, hypertension, high cholesterol, and lack of adequate healthcare. Highly processed and high-fructose corn syrup-laden foods have entered the community's diet at a time when most tribal members are more sedentary than ever. This book is not a substitute for healthy daily food choice or culturally-relevant dietary planning. Poor food choice and lack of exercise are leading causes of bad health. But a simple phrase from our elders is also instructive: "[good] food [can also be] good medicine."

Modified Foods

Modified diabetic and healthy recipes offer an alternative to unhealthy high-processed foods (microwave dinners, can foods and fast foods) and high-fat traditional foods. Before Europeans came, the community's American Indian ancestors ate more fresh fruits, and vegetables and nuts, more lean meats, smaller meat portions, and did far more exercise. These are still key elements to a healthier lifestyle. Traditional foods can be modified to increase nutrients, lower saturated fats, decrease processed sugars, and decrease calories.

Some suggestions:

1. Use smaller portions of fats, sugars, and salt. Decrease portions of meat and breads and increase portions of vegetables.
2. Buy fresh foods or grow your own!
3. Use nonstick pans or light amount of cooking spray instead of greased baking pans.
4. Try the following substitutes:[26]
- Grass-fed bison (buffalo) meat, deer meat instead of beef or pork
-ground turkey for ground beef
-whole wheat flour for white flour in baking
-dry beans for canned beans (most canned beans are packed with sodium)

Turkey Tamales
by Dorothy Remedies Schevers, Shreveport, LA

This is a great recipe that can also work with leftover holiday turkey (boiled and ground or shredded). Dorothy has been making turkey, chicken, and beef tamales for over fifteen years. She says that the seasoning is the key, and that if seasoned properly few people can tell.

3 lbs ground turkey (2 lbs ground turkey plus 1 lb turkey sausage) makes 4-5 dozen.
1 medium onion
4 heaping tablespoons of minced garlic
4-5 dozen corn husks

Spices for your personal taste (chili powder, cayenne pepper, salt, black pepper, cumin, oregano, etc)
Saute onion and garlic in large pan with meat, adding pepper and other spices, season to taste.

For dough, use store-bought masa or make as usual, substituting oil (or vegetable shortening) for lard. You can add chicken or turkey stock instead of warm water. Add garlic powder to the dough for additional flavor.

Simple Grilled Corn on the Cob
by Vickie Holbrook (Many, LA)

8-10 fresh whole cobs of corn. Choose nice, full, sweet ears of corn, husks on. Make sure the husks are green and tightly wrapped to the corn, and that the silks aren't dried out.

Soak corn, husks on in water for a minimum of one hour (overnight is best). Be sure not to remove the husks, as they hold in the moisture and keep the corn from burning.

Place onto grill or directly on hot coals, turning as necessary until brown and charred all over. Let cool, remove husks and silk and enjoy!

(A less-healthy alternative is to carefully pull down the husks, remove silks and add herb, lime-cayenne, or garlic butter then carefully covering with husks again.)

Donald Garcie grilling at the 2014 Choctaw-Apache Powwow.
Photo by the author.

Whole Wheat Zucchini Bread
by Dorothy Remedies Scheevers, Shreveport, LA

2 eggs, beaten
1 cup vegetable oil
2 cups sugar
2 tsp vanilla extract
2 cups grated zucchini (or your preferred fruit or vegetable)
2 cups whole wheat flour
1 tsp salt
½ tsp baking powder
1 ½ tsp cinnamon
1 tsp baking soda
½ cup finely chopped walnuts or pecans

Mix all dry ingredients
Eggs, oil, sugar, vanilla in large bowl until mixture is foamy
Add zucchini
Add dry ingredients
Bake in loaf pans for about 1 hour or golden brown at 325.

Healthier Green onions and Eggs
by Joanne Beebe Sepeda

3 bunches of green onions
Dozen eggs
Dash of salt
Non-stick skillet

Cut green onions blades into small pieces (reserve the bulb) Add green onions and cracked eggs to a large bowl
Beat until well-mixed
Pour onto non-stick skillet or griddle at medium heat
As it firms on one side, flip over and cook on the other

Spicy Roasted Pepper Soup
by Vickie Holbrook (Many, LA)

2-3 jalapeño peppers
2 large cloves garlic, unpeeled
olive oil
1 onion, sliced
2 cans tomatoes (or the equivalent of two large frozen tomatoes), drained.
2-3 cups chicken or vegetable stock
salt to taste

Roast pepper and garlic in 450 degree oven, being sure to turn peppers to roast on both sides. . Caramelize the onions in your soup pot, stirring occasionally. Reduce heat to low and cover.

When the garlic and pepper have cooled, peel the garlic and de-seed the pepper. Using a mortar or food processor, coarsely chop both the garlic and pepper. Add the drained tomatoes and process to a coarse puree.

Uncover the soup pot and increase the heat. Add the pepper, garlic and mixture to the cooked onions. Stir and cook until slightly thickened, about 5 minutes. Reduce heat to medium-low and add the stock. Simmer, stirring occasionally. Add salt spices to taste.

Some foods have traditionally been used to treat ailments among the Choctaw-Apache. This list is for purposes of documentation of traditional "folk cures" only. If you need medical assistance, please see your doctor or local clinic. If you are experiencing a medical emergency, call 911.

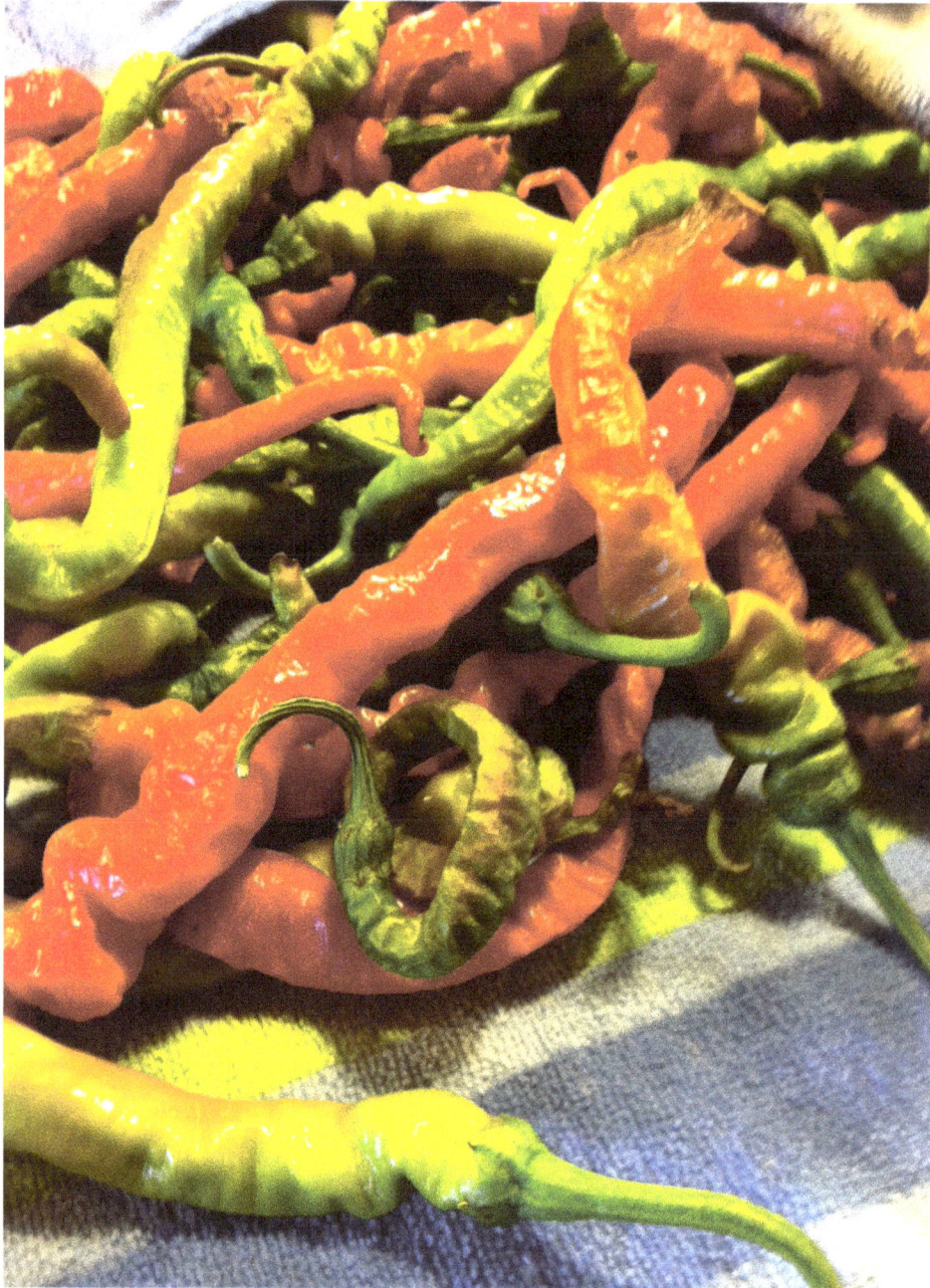

Cowhorn. Photo by the author.

Medicine Foods, As told by John Remedies, Ruby Parrie, and Flora Brown to Rhonda Remedies Gauthier, 1990s

Muscadines, figs, plums, pears - good for blood

All Berries - treats colds, blood pressure, digestion, cysts, sore throat, mouth sores, eyes cataracts

Berry leaves - used to make poultice

Persimmon seeds - colic, stomach

Peppers - circulation, gargle for laryngitis, arthritis, ulcers

Coffee - "makes you smart" (increases alertness)

Corn silk - helps you pee, bladder problems, kidney stones/stomach problems

Apples - stomach, cramps, diarrhea

Black pepper - relieves gas, can also be used for food poisoning

Walnuts, chinkapins, acorns, hickory nuts - cough, constipation and kidney stones. Poultice for sunburns, dandruff, and hair loss

Acorns - (pick up in fall, pound, dry and add to coffee) good for headaches

Rose flowers (rose hips) tea - use little red and pink ones to make tea good for colds, bronchitis, depression, liver also make poultice for skin problems

Hibiscus tea - (red) use for breathing and also a laxative

Polk salad - food, roots make a wash to treat poison ivy before it makes berries

Iris flower blade leaves - use green blades to tie meat up in smoke house (blades did not burn and held meat tight)

Flat cactus leaves - fried or cooked in skillet for lowering cholesterol

Garlic - lowers cholesterol, good for blood pressure, reduce heart attacks

Food Organizing

Over the course of researching and writing this book, I have been part of many discussions of Choctaw-Apache traditional foods. One such conversation occurred on Sunday March 6, 2011, at the VFW Hall in Zwolle. The tribal "covered dish social" featured an initial public presentation of the research for my M.A. thesis project. Joanne Sepeda and Jason Rivers were especially helpful in organizing the event.

Almost fifty people attended the social gathering and public thesis presentation. Foods included tamales, hot water cornbread, chicken, sausage, roasting ear bread, homemade biscuits, greens and turnip dishes, numerous pepper foods, and a few tasty but nontraditional foods, like seafood gumbo.

Joanna Sepeda brought greens, turnip heads (root), roasted chicken, hot water cornbread and green pepper. Gayla Rivers made fry bread. Amelia Bison contributed deer and pork sausage, while Ione Durr brought pig feet and deer sausage. Virginia Malmay made turnip heads and hog jowls and pork and hominy *posole*. Joy Stewart provided chicken and dumplings, cornbread, and pepper. Kenneth Garcie, Christin Leone, and Martha Etheridge offered a variety of pepper dishes. Patsy Ebarb cooked beef tips and rice and corn pudding. Yvonne Busby made pig stew, and Cassie Bison made berry dumplings. The gathering lasted just over two hours and sparked ongoing and wide ranging discussions of the importance of foodways in the community.

Demonstration Garden

The idea for a Spring 2011 demonstration garden came about from discussions I had with Chief John W. Procell, who is himself a gardener, and my mother, Vickie Holbrook, who is a tribal member, master gardener and licensed horticulturalist. John Rogers, a citizen of the United Houma Nation and now retired District Conservationist and American Indian/ Alaska Native Emphasis Program Manager for the USDA/ Soil Conservation District living in Many, Louisiana, has been an advocate of heirloom seeds and also the idea of a demonstration garden.[27]

In late January 2011, Chief John W. Procell burned the ground in the area of the intended garden. In February 2011, Mr. Johnny Lee Rivers, a prolific gardener and member of the tribe, agreed to help with a garden and quickly broke ground at the intended garden location.

I compiled a crop list and began investigating sources from local seed savers, organic and heirloom seed companies, and American Indian seed banks. Some tribal member gardeners are seed savers, but most save "exotic" seeds, and I was unable to find sufficient heirloom seeds for all traditional crops. The Choctaw-Apache tribe is situated at the cultural and geographical intersection of American Indian southeastern, southwestern, and plains cultures. Native Seeds/ SEARCH (www.nativeseeds.org) is committed to seeds traditionally grown in the American Southwest and Mexico. The nonprofit organization is a one stop shop for culturally-relevant seeds grown in the U.S. southwest and Mexico. At the time of this research there was no single native seed bank for the southeastern cultural region. The researcher filled this gap with seeds from sources focusing on heirloom seeds from the southeastern United States and from saved heirloom seeds obtained with the help of John Oswald Colson from adjoining Natchitoches Parish's "downriver" (Cane River Creole) community. On March 31, 2011, Chief Procell, Johnny Lee Rivers, Kenneth Garcie, and a few members of the tribe gathered to plant the garden. The demonstration garden provided a few vegetables to those who worked it, and plenty of seeds to offer to tribal members interested in planting a garden the following year. The modest experiment demonstrated that the tribe can successfully operate a community garden in the future.

Let's Talk Food

Some food terms, phrases and descriptors
Word list from John Remedies complied by Rhonda Remedies Gauthier

corn-mas [Spanish Maize from Taino word Maiz]

peas-frejoles [frijoles Spanish, beans; chícharos are pea]

meal-meleno [from Spanish molino mill]

flour-meleno-triego-thriego [from Spanish trigo wheat]

salt-sal [Spanish]

sugar-sucra [French sucre or Spanish azúcar]

meat-cardnae [Spanish carne]

deer-diea [English "deer"?]

bird-paharo [Spanish pájaro*]

turtle-tartugas [Spanish tortuga, tortose]

red-ruje [French, rouge]

"Freholes is peas. Pecante is pepper. Conye is meat, Pandemaisor pendemonli was cornbread. Pandelus was sweet bread."

— Mrs. Bass, Fred Leone, and Gertrude Castie Leone,
1983 Ebarb Community Collection CHRC

Some Choctaw-related food words used in the community

Kafioshi (Café o shi) [See also Kaf auashli] - Parched coffee, acorn coffee

Minti (ho minty) - "Come home." Used to call children home to eat or come home at night.

Taboki (Taboki baha) - Used as part of sawmill sign language for time to knock off and eat

Kokani - Guineafowl

Portable Seed Bank, 2012. Photo by the author.

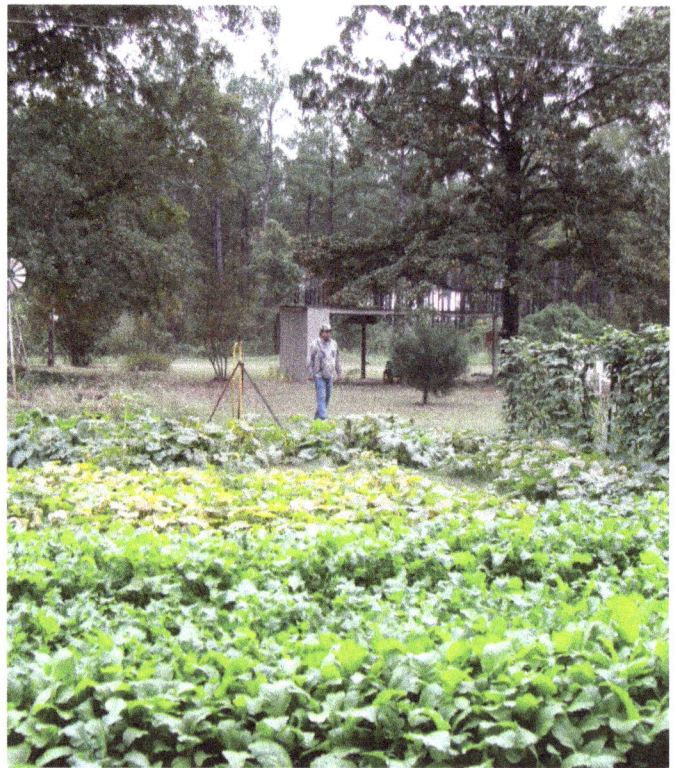

Chief Procell's Garden, 2010. Photo by author.

Male elders and supporters at food event. Photo by the author.

Conclusion

The research revealed a wealth of food-related intangible cultural resources located within the collective conscious of the community. There is a high degree of cultural continuity, amidst cultural change. The community continues to make tamales from scratch, including homemade *masa*, despite it being commercially-available and *nixtamalization* being a labor intensive process. To them, authentic tamales must be made from scratch, even if the corn is not ground with a *metate* like their great-grandparents or a hand grinder like their parents used.

Younger members of the community continue to hunt and fish because they enjoy doing so, and because it allows them to overcome a division with nature. When some men of the community kill a buck in the early winter, they are continuing a long tradition by processing deer into sausage and smoking it in one of the few remaining smokehouses in the area. The food is often shared widely amongst family members and friends, despite the availability of freezers.

Food is a key ingredient in Choctaw-Apache identity, both past and present. Food is closely linked with tradition, family, and home. According to Amelia Bison, many families keep pepper in the refrigerator and eat it daily. For others, traditional foods are not eaten every day, but serve as feast foods. This is most evident at the many family reunions held annually in the summer months and early fall. At these reunions families share food, and the elders recollect a time when the community was more based in subsistence farming and hunting, when food choices were less market dependent and when small clusters of families exercised collective usufruct of a plentiful environment.

The tribe and community no longer exercise a high degree of food sovereignty. That is to say, although traditional foods are important to many people, indeed, an element of their identity, they no longer collectively define or administer their own food, agriculture, livestock and fisheries. They are subject to state and local laws as well as regional, national, and international market forces. A major stumbling block to food sovereignty is the lack of political-territorial sovereignty, otherwise known as "federal acknowledgement" or "recognition." The other major challenge is the lack of independent community-based counter-hegemonic institutions like seed banks, community gardens, trade days, and community markets, where the remaining farmers and ranchers can better market their food and where community members are no longer so deeply dependent on multinational corporations and market forces.[28]

Individual members of the tribe have expressed desire for elements of food sovereignty, including interest in heirloom seeds, building seed banks, encouraging gardening, and doing food demonstrations. Many community members have a garden, and some raise chickens, cattle and other livestock. But the Tribal Council has not—to date—conceptualized a holistic program or undergone strategic planning to move toward greater food sovereignty.

None of those interviewed framed their experiences using terms like "alienation," but many lamented the loss of traditional reciprocity. They commented on the lack of community cohesion and noted the reality of dominant corporate culture and younger tribal members' tendency to move away or commute long distances, and to focus on short-term and individual gain over the human needs within the community. Some have expressed deep concerns about the long-term impacts of the destructive capacity of the oil and timber industries, and the dependence on local timber, oil, and gas companies to which many tribal members are beholden to for their livelihoods. A commitment to ongoing tribal gardens and a seasonal market would represent an attempt at conscious planning for tribal members' food needs.

Food remains an important part of Choctaw-Apache identity. Many people have mislabeled Choctaw-Apache foodways as "Spanish," erasing the native origins of most of the foods. While late twentieth-century tourist motifs have appropriated the indigenous foods and reinterpreted them, using modern stereotypes of Mexico, the foodways are unmistakably indigenous. They are foods that have undoubtedly incorporated Spanish, African, French, and Anglo-American influences. They have their origins in different pre-invasion peoples of the Americas, but they are unambiguously American Indian.

Food is perhaps the strongest ethnic marker of this American Indian community, both to insiders and outsiders. At one time white oak and pine needle baskets were ubiquitous, but the tribe now lacks a vibrant basket making tradition outside a few persistent practitioners. These days nobody makes horn spoons, and many other traditional crafts are also scarce. Neither the colonial-era Spanish language nor any indigenous language can be heard in everyday conversation. Yet the food traditions of the Choctaw-Apache Tribe remain strong. They are a window to other parts of our culture, and they are a critical link to the past that must be preserved for generations to come. This book is one more contribution toward that effort.

Glossary

American Indian: indigenous peoples of the continental United States (counterparts include Alaska Natives, Native Hawaiians, First Nations, and the indigenous peoples of Central and South Americas).

Acculturation: a culture change process that occurs in a society when it experiences intensive firsthand contact with another society.

Anthropology: the study of human culture.

Apache: Name for several culturally related American Indian groups that formerly ranged from Northern Mexico, Arizona, northwestern New Mexico, Texas, and the southern Great Plains. According to Alice Kehoe (1992), Apache, together with Diné (Navajo) were called "Apachu de Nabajo" by the colonial-period Spanish.

Band: relatively small and isolated kin-ordered group that inhabits a specific territory and may split periodically into smaller extended-family groups that are politically independent.

Casta: Spanish colonial caste system to describe the mixed-race people which appeared in the post-Conquest period, based on "race," and used as a form of social control and to determine a person's importance in society.

Choctaw: a southeastern American Indian culture originating in present-day Mississippi.

Coyote: A racial category in the casta system of the colonial-era Spanish Empire used to denote one parent of American Indian and one parent of mestizo ancestry.

Culture: Learned, shared human behavior.

Cultural loss: the abandonment of a specific practice or trait

Ebarb: An unincorporated community in western Sabine Parish, Louisiana located west of Zwolle and east of Toledo Bend along Louisiana Highway 482. The name Ebarb comes from the surname y'Barbo.

Ethnology: the study of sociocultural practices; ethnographic studies, the study of ethnicity.

Heritage Resources: artifacts, documents, locations, myth and folklore (tangibles and intangibles) which are utilized to support heritage claims.

Heritage: a concept that describes an individual's, or group's, identity, usually based on a series of cultural developments.

History: the study of the past. It relies heavily on written documentation.

Indian Country: Native American communities surrounded by the United States.

Lipan: a southern and eastern Athabascan-specking American Indian culture aboriginal to present-day Texas, New Mexico, and the northern Mexican states of Chihuahua, Nuevo León, Coahuila, and Tamaulipas.

Pepper: (Chile pepper):Fruit of the plant genus capsicum. Name of a number of foods and dishes ranging from thin pepper sauces to gravies, to chunky salsas. Can be made with or without eggs. Peppers are high in vitamin C, and eaten raw as a medicine for arthritis and joint aches.

Masa: Spanish word for dough. For the purposes of this study, finely ground corn dough.

Miscere: A term applied to people of assumed mixed descent, from Latin. See also casta and mestizo.

Mestizo: Spanish word for people of mixed Native American and European descent. A racial category in the casta system of the Spanish Empire used to denote one parent of European and one parent of American Indian ancestry.

Museology: museum studies.

Museum: a place dedicated to displaying and educating interested parties about a particular subject.

Nixtamalization: process for the preparation of maize (corn) in which it is soaked and cooked in an alkaline solution (ash or limewater), and hulled. This process is used to make hominy, masa, and tamales and increases the nutritional value of the corn.

Oral History: a field of history that collects the spoken word to supplement written documentary evidence of the past or to offer insight in areas, that lack such documentation.

Tamale: A food made from a starchy corn dough (masa) steamed or boiled in a corn shuck. The wrapping is discarded before eating. Tamales are usually filled with pork or some other meat, but can have almost any, or no, filling.

Tribal Consultation: Communication between the tribe and any other party or parties. Usually refers to a process of communication and collaboration between tribal governments and agencies on one hand and corporate or U.S. government and its agencies on the other.

Bibliography

American Association for State and Local History. Professional Ethics Statement. http://www.aaslh.org/ethics.htm (accessed December 15, 2011).

Anderson, E.N. 2005. *Everyone Eats: Understanding Food and Culture.* New York: NYU Press.

Andrews, Coleen and Alex Ritzheimer. "Production and Procurement: A Glance at the Foodways of Native America." http://uwf.edu/tprewitt/sofood/native.htm (accessed July 23, 2010).

Arden, Traci. 2004. "Where are the Maya in Ancient Maya Archaeological Tourism?: Advertising and the Appropriation of Culture." In Yorke Rowan and Uzi Baram, eds. *Marketing Heritage: Archaeology and the Consumption of the Past.* Walnut Creek, CA: AltaMira Press, 103-113

Avery, George. 1997. Los Adaes Station Archaeology Program 1997 Annual Report. Natchitoches: Northwestern State University.

Barth, Fredrik. 1969. *Ethnic Groups and Boundaries: The Social Organization of Culture Difference.* Boston: Little, Brown and Company.

Booker, Dennis. 1973. *Indian Identity in Louisiana: Two Contrasting Approaches to Ethnic Identity.* M.A. thesis, Baton Rouge: Louisiana State University.

Beresford, Melissa. "Am I a Marxist? Food and Issues of Class" Mundane Ethnography Blog. http://www.mundaneethnography.com/2008/07/am-i-marxist-food-and-isues-of-class.html (accessed April 9, 2011).

Berzok, Linda Murray. 2005. *American Indian Food. Food in American History Series.* Westport, CT: Greenwood Press.

Bittermann, Vanessa. 2007. *Civic agriculture: An Analysis of Citizen and Community Engagement in Vermont's Food System.* MA thesis. Medford, MA: Tufts University.

Bloch, Marc Léopold Benjamin. 1953. *The Historian's Craft.* New York: Vintage Books.

Bolton, Hebert Eugene. 1915. *Texas in the Middle Eighteenth Century.* Berkeley: University of California Press.

Bolton, Hebert Eugene. 2010 (1914). *Athanase de Mézières and the Louisiana-Texas Frontier, 1768-1780: Documents Pub. for the First Time, from the Original Spanish and French Manuscripts, ... of Mexico and Spain; Tr. Into English.* New York: Arthur Clark.

Brooks, James F. 2002. *Captives and Cousins: Slavery, Kinship, and Community in the Southwest Borderlands.* Chapel Hill: University of North Carolina Press.

Buchanan, Carol. 1997. *Brother Crow, Sister Corn: Traditional Native American Indian Gardening.* Berkeley, CA: Ten Speed Press.

Caduto, Michael J. and Joseph Bruchac. 1996. *Native American Gardening: Stories, Projects, and Recipes for Families.* Golden, Colorado: Fulcrum Publishing Company.

Caldwell, Robert. 2011. *Foodways of the Choctaw-Apache Community*. MA thesis. Natchitoches, LA: Nortwestern State University.

Castille, George Pierre and Gilbert Kushner, eds. 1981. *Persistent People: Cultural Enclaves in Perspective*. Tucson: University of Arizona Press.

Chang, Haewon. 2008. *Autoethnography as Method*. Walnut Creek, CA: Left Coast Press.

Chang, K.C. 1977. *Food in Chinese Culture. Anthropological and Historical Perspectives*. New Haven and London: Yale University Press.

Choctaw Apache Tribe of Ebarb and Sabine Parish School District. 2010. Native American Culture Day. (Color Booklet). Self-Published with assistance of Title VII Indian Education Funds: Zwolle, LA.

Cobb, Amanda J. nd. "Powerful Medicine: The Rhetoric of Comanche Activist LaDonna Harris." *SAIL* 18 (4) 63-85.

Cox, Beverly and Martin Jacobs. 1991. *Spirit of the Harvest: North American Indian Cooking*. New York: Stewart, Tabori & Chang.

Cornell, Stephen. 1988. "The Transformations of Tribe: Organization and Self-concept in Native American Ethnicities." *Ethnic and Racial Studies*. 11(1) 27-46.

Crust, Louis 2003. "Sentimental Jamboree: an Exploratory Study of Volunteer Activities at a Farmers' Market" *Volunteer Action Journal*. 6 (1)

Cushing, Frank Hamilton. 1920 [1884-1885]. *Zuni Breadstuff*. New York: Heye Foundation.

David, James P. Jr. 1997. *A Study of American Indian Ethnic Identity and Federal Recognition in the Louisiana Apalachee, Caddo Adais, and Choctaw Apache of Ebarb*. B.A. thesis. Natchitoches, LA: Louisiana Scholars' College at Northwestern State University.

De Caro, Frank. 2009. "Legends, Local Identity, and a New Orleans Cookbook." *Louisiana Folklore Miscellany*. (19) 23-31.

Deloria, Jr., Vine. 1969. *Custer Died for Your Sins: An Indian Manifesto*. Norman: University of Oklahoma Press.

Diehl, Belinda Sue. 2008. *Briarwood, The Caroline Dormon Nature Preserve: Inventory and Display Panels*. M.A. thesis. Natchitoches, LA: Northwestern State University of Louisiana.

Durr, Lisa Sepulvado. 1992. "Folk Cures in the Ebarb Commuunity of Louisiana" *Louisiana Folklife Journal*. Natchitoches, LA: NSU.

Erdrich, Heidi E. "Guidelines for the Treatment of Sacred Objects" *Museum Anthropology*. 33 (2) 249-250.

Fabre, Geneviève et al. (eds.) 2001. *Celebrating Ethnicity and Nation: American Festive Culture from the Revolution to the Early Twentieth Century*. New York: Berghahn Books.

Faine, John R. and Hiram F. Gregory. 1986. The Apache-Choctaw of Ebarb: An Assessment of the Status of a Louisiana Indian Tribe. Baton Rouge: The Institute for Indian Development.

Fine, Elizabeth and Jean Speer. (eds.) 1992. *Performance, Culture, and Identity*. Westport, Connecticut: Praeger.

Folse, John D. 2004. *Encyclopedia of Cajun & Creole Cuisine*. Gonzales, LA: Chef John Folse & Co.

Folse, John D. 2007. *After the Hunt: Louisiana's Authoritative Collection of Wild Game & Game Fish Cookery*. Gonzales, LA: Chef John Folse & Co.

Folse, John D. 2009. *Hooks, Lies & Alibis*. Gonzales, LA: Chef John Folse & Co.

Foster. John Bellamy. 2000. *Marx's Ecology: Materialism and Nature*. New York: Monthly Review Press.

Funari, Pedro Paulo. 2006. "The World Archaeological Congress from a Critical and Personal Perspective." Archaeologies: Journal of the World Archaeological Congress 2 (1) 85-95.

Fuqua, Dustin. 2007. *Anumka Hopaki: Saving A Part of Our Past Planning a Cultural Center for the Jena Band of Choctaw Indians in Louisiana*. M.A.thesis. Natchitoches, LA: Northwestern State University of Louisiana.

Galán, Francis X. 2006. *Last Soldiers, First Pioneers: The Los Adaes Border Community on the Louisiana-Texas Frontier, 1721-1779*. Ph,D. diss., Southern Methodist University.

Geertz, Clifford. 1973. *The Interpretation of Cultures*. New York: Basic Books.

Green, Rayna. "Mother Corn and the Dixie Pig: Native Food in the Native South." *Southern Cultures* 15:4 (2009).

Greenbaum, Susan D. 1985. "In Search of Lost Tribes: Anthropology and the Federal Acknowledgment Process." *Human Organization*. 44 (4) 361-367.

Gregory, H.F. "Pete." 2002. "España y La Louisiana." "Louisiana, Bienvenidos a Todos." Natchitoches, LA: 2002 Louisiana Folklife Festival. http://www.louisianafolklife.org/LT/Articles_Essays/espana_la.html (accessed July 15, 2010).

Guillory, Charles M. 1997. *Soil Survey of Sabine Parish, Louisiana*. Washington, D.C.: United States Department of Agriculture, Natural Resources Conservation Service.

Gulliford. Andrew. 2000. "Native Americans and Museums: Curation and Repatriation of Sacred & Tribal Objects." *Sacred Objects and Sacred Places: Preserving Tribal Traditions*. Boulder: University of Colorado Press. 41-66.

Gutierrez, C. Paige. 1992. *Cajun Foodways*. Jackson, MS: University Press of Mississippi.

Gupta, Akhil and James Ferguson. 2001. *Culture, Power, Place: Explorations in Critical Anthropology*. Durham: Duke University Press.

Hjalager, Anne-Mette and Greg Richards. (eds.) 2002. *Tourism and Gastronomy*. London: Routledge.

Hufford, Mary, ed. 1994. *Conserving Culture: A New Discourse on Heritage*. Chicago: University of Illinois Press.

Jaimes, Annette M. 1992. "Federal Indian Identification Policy: A Usurpation of Indigenous Soverignty in North America." *Native Americans and Public Policy*. Ed. Fremont J. Lydon and Lyman Legters. Pittsburg, PA: University of Pittsburgh Press. 113-135.

Jamison, Cheryl Alters and Bill Jamison. 1995. *The Border Cookbook : Authentic Home Cooking of the American Southwest and Northern Mexico.* Boston: Harvard Commons Press.

Jenkins, Gwinn. 2008. *Contested Space: cultural heritage and identity reconstructions.* Berlin: LIT Verlag.

Kammen, Michael G. 1993. *Mystic Chords of Memory: The Transformation of Tradition in American Culture.* New York: Vintage Books.

Kavasch, E. Barrie. 2005 [1977]. *Native Harvests: American Indian Wild Foods and Recipes.* Mineola, NY: Dover Publishing.

Kehoe, Alice B. 1992. *North American Indians.* Upper Saddle River, NJ: Pretence-Hall.

Kimball, Yeffe and Jean Anderson. 1965. *The Art of American Indian Cooking.* New York: Lyons Press.

King, Thomas F. 2003. *Places that Count: Traditional Cultural Properties in Cultural Resource Management.* Walnut Creek, CA: AltaMira Press.

Kniffen, Fred B. 1968. *Louisiana: Its Land and People.* Baton Rouge: Louisiana State University Press.

Kniffen, Fred B., Hiram F. Gregory and George A. Stokes. 1994 [1978]. *The Historical Indian Tribes of Louisiana From 1542 to the Present.* Baton Rouge: Louisiana State University Press.

Lee, Dayna Bowker. n.d. "Making Tamales in Northwestern Louisiana." http://www.nsula.edu/regionalfolklife/Tamales/default.html (accessed July 15, 2010).

Lee, Dayna Bowker. 1990. *Cultural-historical background for the Apache-Choctaw of Ebarb.* N.p.: n.p. .

Levi-Strauss, Claude. 1966. *The Raw and the Cooked. Introduction to a Science of Mythology, Volume 1.* London: Penguin Press.

Levi-Strauss, Claude. 1973. *From Honey to Ashes. Introduction to a Science of Mythology, Volume 2.* New York: Harper and Rowe.

Loukaki, Argyro. 1997. "Whose Genius Loci?: Contrasting Interpretations of the 'Sacred Rock of the Athenian Acropolis.'" *Annals of the Association of American Geographers,* Volume 97 (2) 306-329.

Lovegren, Sylvia 2005. *Fashionable Food: Seven Decades of Food Fads.* Chicago: University Of Chicago Press.

Lowenthal, David. 1998. *The Heritage Crusade and the Spoils of History.* Cambridge: Cambridge University Press.

Lurie, Nancy Oestreich Lurie and Stuart Levine. 1968. *The American Indian Today.* eland, FL: Everett/ Edwards.

Magness, P.J. 1973. *Evidence supporting the theory of Spanish-American culture in Sabine Parish.* MA thesis. Natchitoches: Northwestern State University.

Marx, Karl. 1887. *Capital: A Critique of Political Economy.* New York: L.W. Schmidt.

McCorkle, James L. 1981. "Los Adaes: Outpost of New Spain." *Journal of the North Louisiana Historical Association* (12). 113-122.

McCorkle, James L. 1984. "Los Adaes and the Borderlands Origins of East Texas." *East Texas Historical Journal* (22).

McCorkle, James L. "Los Adaes" Handbook of Texas Online http://www.tshaonline.org/handbook/online/articles/nfl01 Austin: Texas State Historical Association. (accessed March 15, 2011).

McGraw, A. Joachim. 1998 (1991). *A Texas legacy, the Old San Antonio Road and the caminos reales : a tricentennial history, 1691-1991.*

Mihesuah, Devon A. 1996. *American Indians: Stereotypes & Realities.* Atlanta, GA: Clarity Press.

Mihesuah, Devon A. 2005. *So you want to write about American Indians? A Guide for Writers, Students and Scholars.* Lincoln: University of Nebraska Press.

Mihesuah, Devon A. ed. 1998. *Natives and Academics: Researching and Writing about American Indians.* Lincoln: University of Nebraska Press.

Miller, Jay. 1997. *American Indian Foods.* A True Book. New York: Children's Press.

Motzafi-Haller, Pnina. 1997. "Native Anthropologists and the Politics of Representation." Deborah Reed-Danahay, ed. Auto/ethnography: *Rewriting the Self and the Social.* Oxford: Berg Publishers. 169-195.

Nabhan, Gary Paul., 1989. *Enduring Seeds: Native American Agriculture and Wild Plant Conservation.* Tucson: University of Arizona Press.

Nagel, Joane. 1996. *American Indian Ethic Renewal: Red Power and the Resurgence of Identity and Culture.* New York: Oxford University Press.

Nardini, Louis Raphael. 1961. *No Man's Land: A History of El Camino Real.* New Orleans: Pelican Publishing Company.

Narayan. Kirin. 1993. "How Native is a Native Anthropologist?" *American Anthropologist*, New Series, 95 (3): 671-686.

Nicholas, George. ed. 2010. *Being and Becoming Indigenous Archaeologists.* Left Coast Press, Walnut Creek, CA.

Mandel, Ernest and George Novack. 1970. *The Marxist Theory of Alienation.* New York: Pathfinder Press.

Owens, Maida. 2000. "Louisiana's Food Traditions: An Insider's Guide." http://www.louisianafolklife.org/LT/CSE/creole_food_trad.html (accessed July 15, 2010).

Paredes, Américo. Bauman, Richard, ed. 1993. *Folklore and Culture on the Texas-Mexican Border.* Austin: University of Texas Press

Pierotti, Stephanie, Tammy Bailes, Amy Malmay Parrie, Daniel Parie and Kimerly Schoth. 1996. *Traditional Arts and Crafts in the Choctaw-Apache Community of Ebarb.* Baton Rouge: State of Louisiana Department of Culture, Recreation and Tourism.

Price, Richard. 1983. *First Time: The Historical Vision of an Afro-American People.* Baltimore and London: The Johns Hopkins University Press.

Prins, Harald E.L. 1996. *The Mi'kmaq: Resistance, Accommodation and Cultural Survival.* Ft. Worth, TX and New York: Harcourt Brace Publishers.

Ramirez, Dominica Dominguez. 2004. *Travels in Louisiana: Journeys into Ethnicity and Heritage by two Hispanic Groups.* M.A. thesis, Louisiana State University, Baton Rouge, Louisiana.

Reséndez, Andrés. 2004. *Changing National Identities at the Frontier: Texas and New Mexico, 1800-1850.* Cambridge and New York: Cambridge University Press.

Richards, Marie R. 2010. *Tell Our Story: Collaborating with the Jena Band of Choctaw on Historical Preservation.* M.A.thesis. Natchitoches, LA: Northwestern State University of Louisiana.

Ritchie, Donald A. 2003. *Doing Oral History, A Practical Guide.* New York: Oxford University Press.

Rivers, Marie Lucile and Travis Ebarb Jr. 2007. *Around Ebarb and Toledo Bend. Images of America.* Arcadia, CA: Arcadia Publishing.

Roche, Joan M. 1982. *Sociocultural aspects of diabetes in an Apache-Choctaw community in Louisiana.* Ann Arbor: University Microfilms International.

Sahagún, Bernardino de. 2011. *Historia general de las cosas de la Nueva España II.* Barcelona: Linkgua,

Sauer, Carl O. 1925. "The Morphology of Landscape." *University of California Publications in Geography* 2 (2):19-53. Berkeley: University of California.

Sepulvado, Donald Lester. 1977. "Folk Curing in a Spanish Community." *Louisiana Folklife Journal.* Natchitoches, LA: NSU.

Shoemaker, Janet. 1988. *The "Broken" Spanish of Ebarb: A Study in Language Death.* M.A. thesis, Louisiana State University, Baton Rouge, Louisiana.

Smith, Linda Tuhiwai. 1999. *Decolonizing Methodologies: Research and Indigenous People.* New York: St. Martin's Press.

Spradley, James P. 1980. *Participant Observation.* New York: Holt, Rinehart and Winston.

Spitzer, Nicholas R. (ed.) 1977. *Louisiana Folklife: A Guide to the State. Louisiana Folklife Program/Division of the Arts.*

Tengan, Ty Kawika. 2001. "Reclaiming Space for an Indigenous Anthropology: Some Notes from Social Sciences Building 345" Public Anthropology: The Graduate Journal. Manoa, Hawaii: University of Hawai'i.

Thompson. Richard H. 1989. *Theories of Ethnicity: A Critical Appraisal.* New York: Greenwood Press.

Tilden, Freeman. 1977 [1957]. *Interpreting Our Heritage.* 3rd Ed. Chapel Hill: University of North Carolina Press.

Trimble, Charles E., Barbara W. Sommer, and Mary Kay Quinla. 2008. *The American Indian Oral History Manual: Making Many Voices Heard.* Walnut Creek, CA: Left Coast Press.

Tyler, Lyon Gardner. 1907. Ed. *Narratives of Early Virginia, 1606-1625, Vol. 5.* New York; Charles Scribner and Sons.

UNESCO. 2003. Convention for the Safeguarding of the Intangible Cultural Heritage. Paris: UNESDOC. http://unesdoc.unesco.org/images/0013/001325/132540e.pdf (accessed December 12, 2010).

UNESCO. 2005. Towards Knowledge Societies. UNESCO World Report. Paris: UNESCO. http://unesdoc.unesco.org/images/0014/001418/141843e.pdf(accessed December 12, 2010).

UNESCO. 2010. "Traditional Mexican cuisine - ancestral, ongoing community culture, the Michoacán paradigm." And "Nomination File Number 00400." Representative List of the Intangible Cultural Heritage of Humanity. Paris: UNESCO. http://www.unesco.org/culture/ich/indexphp?lg=en&pg=00011& RL=00400 (accessed Dec 12, 2010).

Van Rheenan, Mary B. 1987. *Can you tell me who my people are? : ethnic identity among the Hispanic-Indian people of Sabine Parish, Louisiana.* M.A. thesis. Baton Rouge, LA: Louisiana State University.

Vlasich, James A. 2005. *Pueblo Indian Agriculture.* Albuqueque: University of New Mexico Press.

Walker, Herb. 1977. *Indian Cookin'.* Amarillo, Tx: Baxter Lane Co.

Waziyatawin, Angela Wilson, et al, eds. 2007, *For Indigenous Eyes Only: A Decolonization Handbook.* School of American Research Press.

Wilson, Gilbert L. 2005. *Native American Gardening: Buffalobird-Woman's Guide to Traditional Methods.* [originially published in 1917 as "Agriculture of the Hidatsa Indians." Bulletin of the University of Minnesotta. Minneapolis] Mineola, NY: Dover Press.

Wendland, Wendy B. 2006. "Intellectual Property and the Protection of Traditional Knowledge and Cultural Expressions." Barbara T. Hoffman, ed. *Art & Cultural Heritage: Law, Policy and Practice.* Cambridge: Cambridge University Press. 327-339.

Wissler, Clark. 1917. *The American Indian: An Introduction to the Anthropology of the New World.* New York: Douglas C. McMurtie.

Zimmerman, Larry J. 2006. "Liberating Archaeology, Liberating Archaeologies, and the WAC." *Archaeologies: Journal of the World Archaeological Congress* 2 (1) 73-79.

Notes

[1] E.N. Anderson, *Everyone Eats: Understanding Food and Culture* (New York: NYU Press, 2005),125-128

[2] Choctaw-Apache website.

[3] Pierotti et al, 1996. I use Choctaw-Apache community in the singular to emphasize the cohesiveness of the tribe. The community encompasses the tribal population in distinct settlements at Ebarb, Grady Hill, Noble, etc. which transcend and overlap dominant culture settlements, as well as in the towns of Many and Zwolle.

[4] See Chang, Haewon. *Autoethnography as Method.* (Walnut Creek, CA: Left Coast Press, 2008).

[5] Traditional foods and traditional food knowledge (TFK) have been contrasted with convenience foods, "fast foods," and generally mass produced, frozen, or ready-made foods from a can.

[6] Wissler, Clark. *The American Indian: An Introduction to the Anthropology of the New World.* (New York: Oxford University Press, 1922 [1917]), 7.

[7] Linda Murray Berzok, *American Indian Food* (Westport, Conn.: Greenwood, 2005), 35.

[8] Berzok, 2005: xx.

[9] See David Lowenthal, *The Heritage Crusade and the Spoils of History* (Cambridge, U.K.: Cambridge University Press, 1998) and Gwynn Jenkins, Contested Space: Cultural Heritage and Identity Reconstructions.(Berlin: LIT Verlag, 2008).

[10] Michael Kammen, *The Mystic Chords of Memory: the Transformation of Tradition in American Culture*, 1st Vintage Books ed. (New York: Vintage, 1993)

[11] UNESCO 2003, 2005, 2010

[12] Gregory, Hiram F. "Los Adaes, the Archaeology of an Ethnic Enclave." *In Historical Archaeology of the Eastern United States*, ed. Robert W. Neuman. (Baton Rouge: Louisiana State University, 1983) and
Fred B. Kniffen, George A. Stokes, and Hiram F. Gregory, *Historic Indian Tribes of Louisiana: From 1542 to the Present* (Baton Rouge: Louisiana State University Press, 1994), 233.

[13] According to the U.S. Census reports 2008 median household income as $34,786 for Sabine Parish, $43,635 for the State of Louisiana, and $52,029 nationally. In year 2000 (the most current detailed information) the average household income for American Indians in Sabine Parish was approximately 7% below the Sabine Parish average, while the per capita income was less than 79% of the average for the Parish. (Census.gov)

[14] Berzok 2005, 137-138

[15] Gregory, personal communication

[16] See Louis Crust's "Sentimental Jamboree: An Exploratory Study of Volunteer Activities at a Farmers' Market," 2003 and Vanessa Bittermann's "Civic Agriculture: An Analysis of Citizen and Community Engagement in Vermont's Food System."

[17] Some of these corn drinks may have been made from pinole at one time, but nobody in the community was familiar with the word, and the details of this tradition seem to be lost. Kafioshi seems to have been used for both acorn and parched corn coffees.

[18] Ebarb Community Collection Interview #10, October 18, 1982.

[19] Bernardino de Sahagún, *Historia general de las cosas de la Nueva España*, John Smith, in Lyon Gardner Tyler, Ed. Narratives of Early Virginia, 1606-1625, Vol. 5 (New York; Charles Scribner and Sons, 1907), 96. See also "Indian Corn" in Lawton Evans, Luther Duncan, George W. Duncan *Farm Life Readers, Book Four*. Boston: Silver, Burdett & Company, 1916), 315 and *Debow's Review*, Vols 3-4 (New Orleans: Office of Commerical Reivew, 1847), 220. For a contemporary account see modern food historian Sylvia Lovegren's, *Fashionable Food: Seven Decades of Food Fads* (Chicago: University Of Chicago Press, 2005), 33.

[20] In addition to the meat-filled tamale, the Navajo also have Ntsidigo'7 or "kneeldown bread," a fresh corn shuckbread, often called Navajo Tamales.

[21] A.J. Remedies, personal communication.

[22] "Traditional Foods," Fort Sill Apache Tribal History, http://www.fortsillapache-nsn.gov/index. php?option=com_content&view=category&layout=blog&id=6&Itemid=9 (accessed May 20, 2013).

[23] Susan Sepulvado 1983, Ebarb Community Collection, CHRC.

[24] Personal Communication; Rhonda Remedies Gauthier notes.

[25] Personal Communication.

[26] The Mayo Clinic offers a substitution list online at http://www.mayoclinic.com/health/healthy-recipes/NU00585, accessed July 15, 2012.

[27] Mr. Rogers is the author of "Heirloom Seeds: Our Cultural Past" http://www.indigenousseedcenter.org/downloads/American_Indian_Heirloom_Seeds11_01_10.pdf

[28] Seed banks, community gardens, etc., can themselves become ideological tools of dominant culture. From a heritage perspective, they can be placed firmly within the realm of "authorized heritage discourse." Seed banks serve a dual heritage and social problems function, garnering monetary support from institutional sources. Some have argued that community gardens can even serve to draw attention away from demands and overt political struggle of oppressed groups. For the purposes of this research, seed banks, community gardens, and associated institutions are conceptualized primarily as: a.) tools towards toward tribal food sovereignty, b.) means to increase the availability of healthy food in the community, and c.) as a point of re-integration with nature (deep ecology). These institutions should be understood in that context, and evaluated primarily on that basis rather than only through the lens of "heritage."

www.ingramcontent.com/pod-product-compliance
Lightning Source LLC
Chambersburg PA
CBHW051556030426

42334CB00034B/3461